Date Loaned

AP 10'68			
AP 30'68			
MY 17'66			
MR 29'68			
Ap. 16-68			
30			
Re May 17			

SAMUEL BUTLER AND
THE WAY OF ALL FLESH

SAMUEL BUTLER

by

G. D. H. COLE

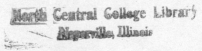
Denver

ALAN SWALLOW

1948

PRINTED BY MORRISON AND GIBB LTD.,
LONDON AND EDINBURGH
BOUND BY THE FRANKLIN BINDERY, CHICAGO

CONTENTS

CHAPTER I

WHO BUTLER WAS

IN Samuel Butler's novel, *The Way of All Flesh*, is cited an essay which the "hero," Ernest Pontifex, is supposed to have contributed to an undergraduate magazine. It contains these words, "It happens that a faithful rendering of contemporary life is the very quality which gives its most permanent interest to any work of fiction, whether in literature or painting." I do not know whether this sentiment was derived from some undergraduate effort of Butler's own, or was written for the purpose of being put into Ernest's mouth : in either case it expresses equally well one of the things that give *The Way of All Flesh* its assured place among English novels, and probably the thing on which Butler would have insisted most strongly if he had been asked to assess the value of his book. Yet "faithful rendering of contemporary life" is only one of the great qualities of Butler's novel, and there are still many who dispute the faithfulness of his presentation. A second quality of the book, plain on the surface, is its satire ; and it is to be admitted that the satirist always in some degree distorts the original. What Butler would have denied is that his satire distorts *more* than any personal record free from all satire would have done. One can imagine—indeed, it is rather fun to imagine—the story of *The Way of All Flesh* written from a quite different point of view—say from that of Ernest Pontifex's (or Butler's) brother or sister. The picture would have been quite different from Butler's picture ; but, had it been a most

" faithful rendering of contemporary life," would it have been nearer the truth, or a good deal farther away ? It would have brought out much that is not brought out in the novel as it is ; but, at least as much, Butler's novel brings out much of which it would have given no inkling. No picture of contemporary life is either the whole truth, or wholly true : every such picture, " whether in literature or painting," is somebody's view of the truth, not the truth itself. It is the satirist's business to get at bits of the truth which the accepted valuations of his contemporaries obscure. That is what Butler did, both in *The Way of All Flesh* and in *Erewhon* and *Erewhon Revisited*. It is a pity that we have not Theobald's or Canon Butler's view of the story, as well as Samuel Butler's ; for the two would make a pretty pair. At all events, what we get in *The Way of All Flesh* is not simply a " faithful rendering of contemporary life," but a satirical rendering—that is, a version written from the standpoint of a set of values which are a long distance away from those of the main characters in the story.

There is a third quality in *The Way of All Flesh*, which gives it, as satire, a special character. The satirist must have positive values of his own : he cannot write good satire if he is merely denying, or scoffing at, the values which most of his contemporaries profess, and appear to accept. He must know where he stands, and must imply, though he need not state, an alternative to what he denies. Mere debunking soon palls—alas, that so many would-be satirists do not know this. The satirist makes his hits, or at any rate keeps them up, only if he is a philosopher as well, in the best and least professional sense of the word. He must know what he likes and approves ; and his likings and approvals must be, not a mere bundle of contrarieties, but a creed that a man can live by.

For what is the point of satire, unless there is a real art of living, and a way of life that does make tolerable sense? Butler believed there was such a way, and did his best to point to it. He was not only a satirist, giving from the satirist's standpoint "a faithful rendering of contemporary life": he was also a constructive critic, trying to tell his contemporaries how to be happier than most of them were.

To be sure, Butler's outlook was limited. Acute critic as he was of many Victorian values, he was very much a Victorian himself. His perception seldom travelled far from the Victorian middle-class home and family; and when it did his view of things became superficial at once. Nothing could well be more thoroughly *bourgeois* than his picture of Erewhonian society; and it is not for being *bourgeois* that Butler mocks at it, for the way of living that he implicitly holds up beside it is not less *bourgeois*. No one ever insisted more firmly than Butler on the Victorian virtue of having enough money to live on securely in a comfortable *bourgeois* way; and no one ever upheld more strongly the importance of prudence—surely the most *bourgeois* of all the virtues. Nor was Butler any less Victorian in his habit of taking the poor for granted—and for that matter the rich as well—and of simply postulating as his norm of good living a middle-class competence that was manifestly outside the reach of the vast majority of men. No doubt, in *The Way of All Flesh*, he made Ernest Pontifex do a number of most un-*bourgeois* things—marry a servant girl who had gone to the bad, keep an old clothes shop, and have his children brought up as bargees. But these were the aberrations of Ernest's wander-years: there was never any doubt of his returning in due course to the fold of a comfortable, *bourgeois* flat.

Of course, the *bourgeoisie* to which Samuel Butler belonged was not the *bourgeoisie* of commerce or industry, but that of the professional class. He was a child of the parsonage, and the grandchild of a schoolmaster who became a bishop ; and the class from which he came regarded itself as belonging to the unquestionable gentry, and took a high standard of education and traditional culture for granted. His class was not the new *bourgeoisie* which had been created by the Industrial Revolution, but rather that middle class which had existed in the eighteenth century and had come through the Industrial Revolution almost unchanged, with a lively sense of its own gentility as contrasted with the vulgarity of many of the new rich, and with a steady allegiance to the Church of England as the church to which all really decent people belonged. The two *bourgeoisies*, that of the old order and that of the new, were still for the most part unfused in Butler's boyhood ; and his associations were essentially with the old *bourgeoisie*, of the liberal professions, and not with the new *bourgeoisie* of trade and industry, though he and his family, like many others of his class, were by no means above making money by the appreciation of the value of land that was being built over as the towns spread, and had for the most part almost as keen an eye for the main chance as the new rich.

Butler, of course, could not have satirised the Victorian middle classes half so well if he had not been one of them, in spirit as well as by upbringing in the sense just defined. He got all the more under their skin because he was criticising them from a standpoint which was fundamentally their own. Nothing is more revealing of this than his attitude to his own family. His comments on his upbringing, both in his stories and in his private letters and conversation, were

invariably scathing, and he said again and again quite unfor-
givable things about his relations. But for all that he never
broke with them, or came near to doing so. He kept on
going to stay with his father, whatever hard words he said
about his visits : he kept on corresponding with his sister,
however much he said he disliked her and accused her of
disliking him. Fiercely as he attacked the Victorian family,
its spell was upon him, and he could not even try to throw it
off. Nor could he ever stop worrying about God, even
when he had become fully convinced that God was not
worrying about him. He had most of the Victorian obses-
sions, though he had many of them upside down. That,
indeed, was how he enjoyed having things : witness his life-
long delight in inverting a proverb or a text. "It is better
to have loved and lost than never to have *lost* at all " gave
him the keenest pleasure : his correspondence with Miss
Savage, who shared his taste, is full of such *bon mots* : they
stood happily on their heads at each other, whenever a
chance offered. But to stand on one's head is not to shift
one's ground ; and both Butler and his lady friend stayed
always within the circle of Victorian respectability, even if
they laughed at many of its values. They both preserved
an immense consciousness of being "naughty," whenever
they said anything that Mrs. Grundy would not have liked.
Indeed, they both got no end of enjoyment, not only out of
being, but even more out of feeling, "naughty." Butler said
somewhere that whenever he went home to his family he
had a sensation of being again a child ; but really he did not
need to go home for that. The feeling of the naughty child
stayed with him all his days, and gave his humour its peculiar
quality. Butler was a *gamin* ; and his great bond with Miss
Savage was that they were *gamins* together.

About twenty years ago I was asked to write on Samuel Butler for the *Encyclopaedia Britannica*. I agreed, and was sent a copy of the article which my contribution was to replace. This gave a brief enough account, but made some comment on most of Butler's books, including *Erewhon, The Fair Haven*, his Italian books, his Homeric studies and translations, his work on Shakespeare's Sonnets, and more particularly his four volumes on the theory of creative evolution. At the end it barely mentioned, without any comment, that he had written in addition a novel, *The Way of All Flesh*, which had been published in 1903, after his death. Plainly the writer of the article had no notion that Butler's posthumous novel was of any special interest or importance. Quite possibly, he had not read it ; and if he had, presumably he had not liked it and had formed no conjecture that it was one of the greatest novels in the English language. It was to him no more than one item in Butler's bibliography, set down for the sake of completeness, but calling for no atten- tion in assessing its author's place in the history of either literature or ideas.

No one, of course, could write like that about Butler now ; for *The Way of All Flesh* has become a " classic " and holds a much securer place among the " classics " than *Erewhon*, which was mainly the source of such fame as he had, outside a small body of admirers, in his own day. All the books he published in his lifetime, with the single exception of *Erewhon*, were commercial failures : he made nothing, or a good deal less than nothing, out of them, and was mostly compelled to publish them at his own expense. Even *Erewhon*, though it was several times reprinted, was never near being a best-seller ; and if its author had depended on writing for his livelihood, he would have sheerly starved.

Fortunately for himself and for posterity, Butler had private means, though they were for a long time straitened ; for he could assuredly never have written anything except just what he wanted to write, and the world would have been the poorer if he had been forced to make his living in some other way.

Actually, Butler did for a time earn his living in New Zealand as a sheep-farmer, before he settled down first to painting and then to writing ; and his first book, *A First Year in Canterbury Settlement*, was put together by his father out of his letters home. Canterbury was then a new settlement, just being opened up for sheep-farming, and Butler did well for himself. The yield of money was high, and he started with the advantage of having enough capital advanced by his father to buy and stock a farm, after he had learnt the trade. With this start, provided that he showed reasonable industry and competence, he had every chance to prosper ; and his property grew fast in value, besides yielding him an adequate income. But Butler had no intention of spending his life as a sheep-farmer ; and after five years in New Zealand he felt rich enough to sell out and return home. He had made a sum which, invested in good securities, seemed likely to yield him as much as he wanted for the kind of life he had it in mind to lead.

Butler's ambition at this time was to become a painter, and it was to painting that he gave his main attention for some time after his return to England in 1864. He took his art seriously, and from 1868 until 1876 was an occasional exhibitor at the Royal Academy and at other " shows." Some of his paintings have considerable, though none tran- scendent, merit ; but when he turned aside from painting to literature and published *Erewhon* in 1872 he still regarded his writing as no more than a side-line. He had written squibs and essays at Cambridge as an undergraduate, and in New Zealand had contributed to *The Press*—a journal of some literary pretensions in the new colony, which rather prided itself on its culture : indeed, the first adumbration of *Erewhon*, later incorporated in *The Book of the Machines*, made its original appearance in this journal. This writing, however, had been merely occasional, and it took the success of *Erewhon* to turn him towards regular book-writing. *The Fair Haven*, which had its germ in an anonymous pamphlet which he had written some time before in the process of resolving his doubts about Christian evidences, appeared in 1873—the year after *Erewhon* ; and no sooner was that done than, encouraged by his faithful friend, Miss Savage, he set to work on the first draft of *The Way of All Flesh*. He was still, however, as his correspondence with Miss Savage shows, very doubtful of his capacity as an author. He was half uncertain of having enough to say, and half hesitant about how far he was prepared to go in outraging current conventions. Painting still seemed to him to be the first thing ; and the contest continued for some years before he began to feel sure that he could not both paint and write well, and, gripped by an idea that he could not let alone, gradually pushed painting aside and took to regular writing. Butler never ceased to paint, for his own satisfaction ; but after the middle 'seventies he painted only to please himself.

The Way of All Flesh was first written while he was in this transitional phase, and as he wrote it the chapters passed to and fro between him and Miss Savage, who admired them greatly and continually urged him on. He published nothing between *The Fair Haven* in 1873 and *Life and Habit*—his first book on creative evolution—in 1877 ; but in 1876 he exhibited his last Royal Academy picture, and from that point he turned decisively towards writing. The series of books on evolution, in which the ideas put forward in *Life and Habit* were developed and his critics answered, diverted him for a time from story-telling, and he went back to his novel only in the early 'eighties, after he had written not only *Evolution New and Old* and *Unconscious Memory*, but also *Alps and Sanctuaries*, in which he first recorded his love of Italy and of primitive Italian art. Thereafter he worked again for a year or two over the manuscript of his novel, rewriting much of it ; but presently he again laid it aside, having made up his mind against publication while many of the real people from whom he had drawn his characters were still alive. He said again and again that he meant to go back to it and to rewrite it all over again ; but he never did. The text remained as he had left it in 1884, and was published, by the decision of his literary executor, the year after his death.

Butler's contemporaries, therefore, knew Butler as a story-teller only by means of *Erewhon*—to which he added *Erewhon Revisited* nearly thirty years later, the year before he died. They knew him mainly as " *Erewhon* " Butler, a curious, cranky writer who had produced, besides his successful satire, a strangely mixed collection of books, in which he almost always appeared to be saying something wilfully perverse. Butler was the man who had denied the story of the Resurrection—not, as David Strauss had done in his *Life of Jesus*, by attributing Christ's supposed reappearances after death to hallucination on the part of his disciples, but by denying the fact of Christ's death upon the Cross—or at any rate by denying that the death could be regarded as proved by the available evidence. Over and above this, Butler was the man who had denied the current scientific doctrine of evolution by natural selection and, not being a trained scientist, had ventured to oppose to it a theory of creative evolution which he professed to have found in the superseded work of Erasmus Darwin (Charles Darwin's grandfather), of Buffon, and of Lamarck. Yet again, Butler was the man who, not being a professional scholar, had declared, not merely that the *Odyssey* was not composed by Homer, but that it had been written by a young woman, who had put herself into the poem as Nausicaa, the daughter of the Phaeacian king ; and, not content with this, Butler was the man who had set out to prove that the *Odyssey* had been composed at Trapani, in Sicily, that its geography was mostly taken from the area round Trapani, and that most of Odysseus's wanderings consisted of a voyage round Sicily. Besides all this, Butler was the man who had put forward some very unorthodox views about Italian painting and about music—he even regarded Handel as the world's greatest composer, and had tried to compose music in Handel's style. He had written an unconvincing book about Shakespeare's sonnets—thereby ranging himself unquestion-ably among the cranks—and he had produced a very long, very dull, laudatory life of his grandfather, who had been first a headmaster and then a bishop—two callings for which elsewhere he had previously displayed only strong dislike. In short, Butler was a dabbler in many arts and sciences, and no authority upon any. It was conceded that, in *Erewhon*, he had shown for once a pretty wit ; and no doubt there was cleverness, of a sort, in all his writings. But it was agreed that he was not to be taken seriously—the more so, because it was seldom clear whether he meant what he said seriously or not.

Of course, not everyone who thought of Butler at all thought of him in this way. He had devout admirers, in his lifetime, before *The Way of All Flesh* had brought many new admirers to his earlier books. His admirers, moreover, were mostly very intelligent people, and Bernard Shaw was prominent among them, and took Butler's evolutionary theories and also his ideas about education and the family very seriously indeed. But, while Butler lived, his devotees, and even his readers—except for *Erewhon*—were few ; and if most of his books were not out of print, that was rather because there were plenty of unsold copies on hand then because anybody had thought it worth while to reprint them. Butler groused often at his want of commercial success, and was inclined, when he could, to attribute it to sinister causes. He had a particular grievance against the scientists for taking no notice of his theories of memory and creative evolution, and was very ready to suppose that they were all in a conspiracy to discredit him. He was no less angry with the classical scholars for ignoring his theories about Homer ; and in both these connections he threw about quite absurd charges of dishonest dealing. He quarrelled violently with Darwin on the basis of a sheer misunderstanding ; and he fiercely attacked Professor Jebb for saying nothing about his Odyssean theories in a new edition of his *Introduction to Homer* published only six weeks after his account of them had appeared in *The Athenaeum*.

On these, and on other, occasions Butler showed plainly that he had himself a skin too few. It would be going too far to say that he suffered from " persecution mania," even in a mild form ; but he was always unduly ready to believe that other people were trying to thwart him and to run him down. This tendency came, I have no doubt, from his experiences in childhood. He would have it, almost from the beginning, that his father was determined to thwart him at every turn, and later on he had a way of regarding a large part of the world as made in his father's image—or perhaps one should say in the image of the image of his father which he had made. He liked to call himself "Ishmael," and to assert that the whole world of reviewers was against him for the same reason as his father had been against him—that is, out of a dislike of everything unexpected or provocative of thought about things that were supposed to be settled. Up to a point he was of course right, both about his father and about the reviewers ; but he was no more right in the one case than in the other in attributing malice. Canon Butler was simply unable to understand or sympathise with his son's point of view, which seemed to him merely perverse. The reviewers, or a good many of them, felt much the same about Butler's books. One set of paradoxes— *Erewhon*—was amusing enough, and could be treated as a joke ; but what was a poor reviewer to make of an author whose every book was a paradox, and whom they could never tell when to take seriously and when not ?

Besides, from the reviewing end, it stood to reason that Butler must be a dabbler. Biblical criticism was a serious matter, to be reserved for theologians, and not to be treated flippantly, and in pseudo-novelistic form, as Butler treated it in *The Fair Haven*. Or, if Butler had to be accepted as a " higher critic," what business had he to come forward in his next book as a scientist, in flat contradiction of Darwin and of all the best scientific opinion ? Plainly the man was not a real pukka scientist ; and accordingly his views on science were best ignored. Besides, it was quite on the cards that he did not mean what he said : perhaps *Life and*

Habit was, like *The Fair Haven*, just another elaborate hoax. That this time no hoax was intended appeared before long ; for no man could have kept up a hoax through four substantial and closely argued volumes without giving himself away. But, if Butler were serious, all the more reason for ignoring him. Amateurs had no right to advance subversive scientific theories and to expect to be taken seriously. By the time Butler had written four whole books about evolution the reviewers had mostly decided, without reading them, that he was merely yet another bore with a bee in his bonnet. And then, as if he had not done enough to rule himself out of court, he must needs bob up with yet another absurd pretension, and set out to prove that the *Odyssey*, which everyone knew was by Homer, had been written in Sicily by a young lady whose existence nobody had ever suspected before. The classical scholars all knew by instinct that Butler was talking nonsense, just as the scientists had known it when he began refuting Darwin. And, to crown all, this same Butler needs must take to writing books about art and to crying up a painter, called Tabachetti, of whom no real art critic had ever heard, and even to composing half-satirical music in the style of Handel, whom he claimed to be the one truly great composer the world had possessed. All this, moreover, he had done after trying his hand, not very successfully, at painting and exhibiting for a number of years at the Royal Academy, until they would have no more of him. This Samuel Butler was manifestly a crank ; and all wise people know that it is best to leave cranks severely alone—if only they will let you. No one ever got any benefit out of arguing with a crank, because no crank is ever satisfied or ready to stop arguing, or to stop accusing his critics of being in a dishonest conspiracy against him.

Safest, then, it seemed to let Butler alone ; and who can wonder ? It may be the reviewer's greatest glory to discover an unknown genius ; but there is no glory to be got by praising a known and acknowledged crank—at any rate till he is dead and cannot hit back at you for not praising him enough. Butler was dead when *The Way of All Flesh* was published in 1903, and then at length the reviewers were free to discover that he had been a great writer after all.

CHAPTER II

CREATIVE EVOLUTION

SAMUEL BUTLER takes his place among the major British novelists by virtue of a single book—*The Way of All Flesh*. Besides that masterpiece, he wrote but two story-books, *Erewhon* and *Erewhon Revisited* ; and these are hardly more novels than *Gulliver's Travels*. They are satires, first and foremost ; whereas *The Way of All Flesh*, for all its satirical quality, is primarily a story, and therewith a novel in the traditional English manner—discursive, episodic, moralistic, and written in open defiance of all the niceties. I hold it to be one of the great novels, in this mode ; but its greatness is no reason for regretting that the author never attempted another. He had, pure satire apart, just this one novel in him, and no more ; and though he felt dissatisfied with it in the form in which he left it, still unpublished, at his death, it is almost certainly fortunate that he never revised it a second time. Revision, nearly thirty years after, in the softer light of more tranquil rejudgments, would unavoidably have left it less perfect as a " period piece " ; and, for the readers of to-day, a " period piece " it is, both in what it says and in what it leaves unsaid and, quite manifestly, even unthought-of.

A man who revolts against the values of his time and place does not cease to belong to his time and place ; and, as we have seen, Butler, in revolt against so many of the mid-Victorian values, remained eminently a Victorian himself. The things that interested him, the things that roused his opposition, were of his age and country ; and so, no less, were the things that he took for granted, or passed over in silence because they did not interest him at all. There has been so great a shift in this country, of values, of habits, and of interests, that Butler's parables, which went right home, when he made them, to every intelligent person's experience—or would have, if he had published *The Way of All Flesh* soon after writing it—are now in many cases no longer parables at all, but rather pictures of an outmoded past. They no longer shock, or bite, as they would have shocked and bitten then : they are like the reverse side of an old coin, stirring the imagination rather than the memory, and helping us to recreate the past as a living period, and no longer to draw dreadfully exact parallels from our own or from our neighbours' lives.

Samuel Butler was born in 1835, and died in 1902. *Erewhon* was published in 1872 ; and he began writing *The Way of All Flesh* almost as soon as it was finished, and worked at it intermittently, and with long intervals between the spells of activity, until 1884. Thereafter he did no more to it : so that most of the book was written when he was in his forties. The fictitious narrator, Overton, is supposed to have written it, except the last chapter, in or about 1867, as a man in his early sixties, thirty years Butler's senior. The dating is important ; for the entire atmosphere of the narrative belongs to a particular time, and that a time with a very peculiar quality of its own. The years between 1850 and the middle 'seventies have often been called the " golden age " of British capitalism. They were years when wealth not only accumulated fast in the hands of the upper and middle classes, but also began to filter down to the upper strata of the working classes and even, in smaller measure, to the great majority of the people. Because of this, they were years singularly untroubled, save at the very end, by manifestations of acute social discontent. Chartism, the last great boiling up of the continuous unrest of the first half of the century, was over and done with ; and though there was much ado about the agitation which accompanied the contest over the second Reform Act, passed in 1867, and about the rise of Trade Unionism as a force demanding social and legislative recognition, these affairs occupied but a minor place in the attention of the unbusinesslike section of the middle class to which Butler belonged, and in any case came much above the surface only after the date at which his novel was supposed to have been written. Certainly these social struggles made no deep impression on Butler's youthful mind ; and there is barely a reference to them in all his work, or even in his private letters. The " social question," as it has been understood since his earlier books were composed, never aroused his interest. The relations between class and class, or between master and man, were not problems with which his mind was in any way concerned. The greatest and most acute critic of mid-Victorian morality had not a word to say about such things as these. Apart from a few glimpses of " low life," seen as a thing external and vitally different from the life he knew and depicted, Butler's scenes and characters were all of the middle classes, and took middle-class ways of living for granted. In *Erewhon*, as much as in *The Way of All Flesh*, the story moves in a thoroughly *bourgeois* environment. There were working classes in *Erewhon* ; but one hears almost nothing of them. They were simply taken for granted. In this, of course, Butler is not at all singular. Most of the mid-Victorian novelists—except to some extent George Eliot—did for the most part treat the *bourgeois* home and the *bourgeois* way of life as the natural setting for their stories, and did this no less when they were describing " high life " or " low life " than when their actual scenes and characters were of the middle class. No novelist could well be more *bourgeois* than Anthony Trollope ; and Butler differs from him in this respect only in being highly critical of *some*—but by no means of all—the *bourgeois* values, and in not deviating ever into descriptions of a class higher than his own. My point here is that Butler, iconoclast as he was by nature, was always a *bourgeois* idol-smasher, as well as a smasher of *bourgeois* idols. His standards were different from those of other writers of his time, but they were equally *bourgeois* standards. He was far more *bourgeois* than Dickens, or than Thomas Hardy, and quite as *bourgeois* as Charlotte Yonge.

The time when this attitude was most easily taken, with no consciousness of deliberately setting any vital contemporary issue aside, was undoubtedly the time when Butler was gathering the impressions and experiences that he incorporated in *Erewhon* and in *The Way of All Flesh*. The principal event in English history, between the no-event of the English Revolution that did not happen in 1848 and the Reform Act that did happen in 1867, was the publication of Darwin's *Origin of Species* in 1859, the year after Butler had taken his degree at Cambridge. The son of a clergyman, the grandson of a bishop, and himself brought up in the idea that he was to be ordained almost as a matter of course, Butler was to feel as sharply as any man the impact of the new wave of religious doubt that Darwin's book set in motion ; and to him, as to many others, this one issue for a long time seemed to overshadow every other. It was not, however, because of Darwin that he reacted against ordination and resisted his father's pressure that he should allow himself to be made a clergyman without feeling the call. Butler's reaction against Christian orthodoxy came for the most part later than his repudiation of the notion of becoming a parson. Nor was his attack upon orthodoxy ever mainly based on Darwinism, though of course he was influenced by it. Always he disliked strongly the idea of a mechanically determined universe ; and the Darwinian doctrine of natural selection alienated his sympathy because it seemed to make an end of free will as the director of universal affairs. He was unhappy until he had found, or rather rediscovered, a form of the doctrine of evolution that put will, or cunning, rather than luck, in the key place ; and his attack on the Christian theology was scientific only in the sense that he insisted on a strict sifting of the evidence bearing on a matter so vital, if there were any chance of it being true, as the Resurrection of Jesus Christ and the miraculous element in his life and ministry. There is no trace of Darwinism, or of any argument based on natural science, in *The Fair Haven*, which could indeed have been written without a word different if *The Origin of Species* had never appeared. David Strauss and his followers, and " higher critics " of other schools untouched by the Darwinian doctrine, were the inspirers of Butler's religious scepticism.

In *The Way of All Flesh*, on the other hand, and of course in *Erewhon*, the influence of Darwin's theory is plain. In *Erewhon* Butler was still puzzled, not having yet hit on the notion of creative evolution which he proclaimed in *Life and Habit*. In *The Way of All Flesh*, on the other hand, the notions of inherited habit and spontaneous variation by means of willed adaptation to environment are invoked again and again—though probably many of these passages

belong to the period during which he worked over the
original version a second time. Between *Erewhon* and the
revised version of *The Way of All Flesh* Butler had made
his peace with the universe, and had found something to
believe in as well as much to disavow. He made Ernest
Pontifex, in *The Way of All Flesh*, reach after many searchings
the conclusion " that no system which should go perfectly
upon all fours was possible, inasmuch as no one could get
behind Bishop Berkeley, and therefore no absolutely incontrovertible first premise could ever be laid " ; and then
he added of Ernest that " having found this he was just as
well pleased as if he had found the most perfect system
imaginable." This, no doubt, was said in reference to
metaphysical speculation, for which Butler, at any rate after
his first growing pains, never had any use. But he himself
found, if not an " incontrovertible first premise," at any
rate a thoroughly satisfactory working hypothesis ; and
only when he had reached this point did he arrive at a
tranquil adaptation to the mental climate of his age. *Life
and Habit,* and the theory of evolution which he therein
first expressed, were the turning point in Butler's mental
attitude ; and a part of the interest of *The Way of All Flesh*
is that it embodies an imperfect writing of his new positive
view of life into a draft for which a more negative spirit
had furnished the initial inspiration.

The theory of evolution, as Butler looked at it, was not
primarily a scientific theory about animals : it was a practical
working notion about men. Reduced to its simplest
elements, it had two main aspects—inherited memory,
which *was* habit, and " cunning," or will, or striving, in
place of the blind chance of " natural selection," as the
basis of variation and therefore of evolutionary progress.

According to Butler, personality was not a private, mental possession : it was continuous through the ages from generation to generation, each *ego* inheriting the memory of its ancestors and being able to reproduce by inherited habit its ancestors' ways of coping with familiar situations. That was one side of the doctrine : the other side came into play when the *ego* was faced with a new situation to which its inherited memory supplied no valid answer. What happened then ? According to Darwin, there were " variations," of unexplained origin, and those " variations " which the new situation happened to suit survived, whereas the " unfitter " died out. This was " natural selection." According to Butler, what happened was essentially different. The *ego,* faced with the unfamiliar situation, *tried* to adapt itself, and sometimes succeeded, if the gap between the precepts of inherited memory and the needs of the new situation were not too wide. The adaptation, once achieved, became in its turn an inheritable memory, and in course of time a habit. This was Progress, with its Victorian big P ; and, for Butler, the beauty of the theory was that it put back mind and will into the centre of the evolutionary picture, whereas the Darwinians,[1] in the name of scientific necessity, were in fact reducing everything to blind chance. They could not explain " variation " : they treated it as merely an accident and, in making everything depend on it, made chance the sole master of man's fate. This seemed to Butler as unscientific as it was unsatisfying. He wanted a world ruled by laws, not by chance ; and at the same time he wanted man to be the master of his own affairs.

[1] This is not wholly true of Darwin himself ; for in the later editions of *The Origin of Species* he showed an increasing caution on the essential issue whether " natural selection " furnished, by itself, a sufficient explanation of the process of organic evolution.

Variation by " cunning," not by " luck," *plus* unconscious memory, transmitted from generation to generation, gave him the answer he wanted, and he embraced it with enthusiasm.

It is true enough that Butler was no scientist, and that his opinions, *qua* scientist, would not have been worth a rush. But he was not really theorising, except incidentally, about the evolution of animal species : he was thinking about men and women, as he actually met them and mingled with them, and tried to understand their behaviour. His two hypotheses of inherited memory and creative development seemed to him to fit the human facts as he knew them. He saw people behaving in ways which seemed to him intelligible only on the assumption of inherited habit ; for how could they possibly have learned in their own lifetimes to do without conscious effort all the incredibly difficult things, from breathing onwards, which from babyhood they did somehow manage to do ? That was one thing ; and, for another, he constantly saw people trying to handle new situations, often failing, but sometimes succeeding when the required adaptation of familiar behaviour was not too great. If this was the case among men—and he knew it was—why should not the same explanations hold good over the entire field of organic evolution ? No sooner had the idea presented itself than he felt assured of its truth, and certain, though he was no scientist, that the role assigned by Darwin and his interpreters to blind " natural selection " was wrong.

That was how Butler came to run full-tilt into the great Darwinian controversy, while it was still fresh and lively. He would not have cared two straws how species had evolved, or whether they had evolved or not, unless Darwin's theory had carried with it implications about men, not merely in the dim past of the race, but now. But it seemed to him that Darwinism, as far as it rested on the theory of "natural selection," emptied mind out of the universe as a creative force ; and, feeling certain that mind was creative and that men's wills did act with effect, he could not accept Darwinism as valid in the field which he felt he knew something about—the field of everyday human living. If, however, "natural selection" did not hold good there, was there any good reason for supposing that it held good elsewhere ? Butler was impelled to challenge, not simply the applicability of Darwinism to the affairs of civilised man, but the whole theory—for it seemed to him to be all vitiated by its final acceptance of fortuitous, or at any rate of unexplained, variations as the source of progress.

It must be remembered that, when Butler wrote *Life and Habit* and his other books on evolution, Darwinism was by no means simply a scientific doctrine. It was no more so than dialectical materialism is to-day. It was ethics, it was politics, it was theology : it was everything rolled into one. Not that Darwin had "discovered" evolution, or been the first to formulate a theory of it. Theories based on the concept of evolution had been plentiful long before *The Origin of Species* was published. They had been advanced by Buffon, by Lamarck, and by Charles Darwin's grandfather, Erasmus Darwin ; and they had already been built into the framework of philosophical systems, first by Hegel and then by Marx. What Charles Darwin had done was not merely to make out a case for believing in evolution, but to present that case in a form which seemed to leave no room for the action of mind or will in shaping the order of things. This it was, and not evolution as such, that seemed to Butler to empty God and man together out of the course of nature, as creative forces, and to leave only a mindless interaction of law and chance. Chance variations, or " sports," flung into an environment ruled by inexorable laws, survived or perished according to a process of " natural selection " into which neither God's will nor man's nor any being's appeared to enter at all.

This view of the world took many men aback. Some were appalled by it, and rejected the entire evolutionary doctrine because its consequences seemed intolerable to thought. Others rejoiced in it, as administering the final blow to religious superstition. Some found comfort in it, as reinforcing the laws of political economy with a cosmic statement of the theory of perfect competition : some tried to limit it, arguing that it might hold good for mere brute creation, but not for civilised, self-conscious, reasoning and moral man. Almost everyone found in it either what he wanted or what he so disliked as to make him reject it out of hand. Hardly anyone who thought at all could bear to stay neutral. There was a babel of tongues, for and against Darwin—for and against the entire doctrine of the evolution of species. The discoveries of geology had been met, to the satisfaction of a large number of people, by the contention that it was quite within God's power so to create the world as to compress into six days the history of geological ages. The new challenge was much more fundamental ; for could God possibly be supposed to have created a world not subject to the rule of mind, but swept along upon the unguided wheels of chance ?

Many men escaped by sheer rejection of the whole notion of evolution. But Butler could not take this way out. He was entirely convinced that the theory of evolution was sound and that Darwin had done great service by demonstrating its truth, at whatever cost to Christian theology. The theory of evolution itself was sound ; but Darwin had gone wrong in stating it in terms of "natural selection," instead of developing the thought of his grandfather, which had left the influence of mind and will unchallenged. Butler wanted, not to attack Darwin's main doctrine, but to restate it in terms which fitted in better with his own experience and observation. But, because Darwin's theory was *in form* a scientific theory, argued in terms of organic life as a whole—though it was *in effect* fully as much a philosophical theory, bearing on the central conception of human life and purpose—Butler attacked it on Darwin's ground, as science, and not simply on his own ground of human philosophy. I am not suggesting that he made this choice deliberately, knowing an alternative line to be open. He attacked on the scientific plane a doctrine which had been advanced on the scientific plane, though its effects were fully as much human as scientific : he attacked it not because it was bad science, of which he was no judge, but because in his view it was bad human philosophy, and ran counter to the known facts of human experience and behaviour.

The inevitable consequence was a conflict of cross-purposes and misunderstandings. The scientists would have nothing to say to Butler, because he was not one of themselves. Charles Darwin himself urged Dr. Krause, the biographer of Erasmus Darwin, that he should " not expend much powder and shot on Mr. Butler, for he really is not worthy of it. His work is merely ephemeral." What Charles Darwin meant was not so much that he disagreed with Butler as that Butler was inconsiderable as a scientist : he entirely failed to realise that a man who was nothing as a scientist might have something very considerable to say about evolution, because evolution was much more than a scientific concept, in the ordinary meaning of the term " science." Since then scientists, as well as others, have come to see that there was much more in Butler's contentions, even from the strictly scientific standpoint, than Darwin and his adherents would allow at the time. It has been admitted that attributing evolution to " variations " explains nothing, unless we can be told how variations arise. Butler may not have been right in attributing everything to will , or " cunning " ; but he was certainly correct in pointing out that it was a curious sort of science that put down everything in the last resort to chance.

The prolonged argument that runs through Butler's four books on evolution, though cast into a scientific mould, is not really a scientific argument at all, though it of course involves scientific consequences. It is an argument about how men behave, learn, and adapt themselves to the environments with which they have to cope. Its moral, for men's guidance, is that there is in each of us a certain limited power of adaptation, which makes it possible for us to face without disaster, or even with positive benefit, unexpected situations such as neither our inherited memory enables us to deal with unconsciously nor our past experience to cope with easily, by doing again as we have done before. Butler stresses not only that we possess this power of adaptation, but also its limits. If the " cross " is too wide—that is, if the action required of us is too different from what we can do by unconscious habit or by conscious adaptation of habit—we shall fail ; for we cannot act, under any stimulus, more than a little " out of character." It is therefore of the first import-ance for us not to get, if we can help it, into situations which demand too much of us—quite as important as it is to use, when the occasion demands it, all the adaptive powers we do possess.

This, it may be said, is the philosophy of a timid man, and wholly unfit for heroes. So it is. Butler was by nature a timid soul, and never ceased to be afraid of his own deviations from the normal. Almost certainly, this timidity was at the root of his feeling about his father. Whenever Canon Butler tried to influence his son for good, the son was frightened; and his fright gave him the notion that his father was a tyrant, bent on suppressing his son's personality in order to exalt his own. Later, he realised that his father had been timid too: he made Theobald, in *The Way of All Flesh*, as timid by nature as Ernest Pontifex. Indeed, he made Theobald's natural timidity in part the basis of his tyranny; for he understood well enough, from his own character, that timidity is no bar to self-assertion. The timid man can be as obstinate as his naturally brave neighbour; but he saves his soul by running away when he can, and stays to fight only when he is cornered or is quite sure that his antagonist is weaker than himself. Butler, as an author, won a reputation for combativeness, and did not readily run away on paper. He was not afraid of literary combats, in which, he was well aware, neither bones nor fortunes were likely to get broken. But he was timid socially, and in the flesh, with men and women alike; and as soon as he could—that is, from the moment of his return from New Zealand—he built himself as strong a shell as he could devise, and stayed in it for the rest of his life. His shell was his set of bachelor chambers in Clifford's Inn, from which he never removed. He remained unmarried, not because the sexual impulse was weak in him (on the contrary, it was strong and persistent), but because the idea of marriage

3

scared him. He never ceased to be scared that Miss Savage was trying to marry him. Perhaps she was, perhaps she wasn't—it does not affect the point. Butler was scared by his father in childhood, and he stayed scared all his life.

That is the explanation of Towneley—the only quite impossible person in *The Way of All Flesh*. Butler makes Towneley his, and Ernest Pontifex's, ideal man. He makes Ernest say

> "I see it all now. The people like Towneley are the only ones who know anything that is worth knowing, and like that of course I can never be. But to make Towneleys possible there must be hewers of wood and drawers of water—men in fact through whom conscious knowledge must pass before it can reach those who can apply it gracefully and instinctively as the Towneleys can. I am a hewer of wood, but if I accept the position frankly and do not set up to be a Towneley, it does not matter."

By "hewers of wood" Butler does not mean poor men who have to work for the Towneleys' benefit (for Butler as a matter of course made Towneley rich as well as handsome and full of *savoir faire*) : he means people who have to learn good habits in order to transmit them as "unconscious memories" to their children's children. Towneley is Butler's version of the superman, gifted by instinct, which is "unconscious memory" with all the attributes of serenity and good manners that enable him to confront his environment without fear or shrinking. Towneley is his Greek god in modern dress ; and because he is modern he has made his property a part of his unconscious personality. He is not conscious of being rich, or of administering largesse : he is rich and generous by heredity and instinct. He is indeed so immaculate a conception that the reader—or at any rate this reader—takes a strong dislike to him as soon as he appears on the stage.

Next to the Towneleys—Butler mistook Pauli, of whom more presently, for a potential Towneley, and thought he ought to be rich—next to the Towneleys, Butler admired good-looking Italian peasants, who did not bother their heads about the universe and seemed to him, though poor in a sense, perfectly adapted to their sunlit environment. He was very much at the mercy of good looks, at any rate in men, all the days of his life. He liked strong, upstanding, careless men, who got the most out of life without fussing. He contrasted such men with himself, and knew himself to be neither beautiful nor upstanding nor careless, but possessed of a tendency to fuss which he was always trying to keep in check in his personal affairs, while he gave it full freedom to range in literary adventures. His own habits were not free and careless, but carefully protective. He was in fact forming them not, like Ernest, for his children's children, but for his own safe-keeping in a dangerous world. But, significantly, though he modelled Ernest Pontifex after himself, he gave his " hero " children, and saw to it that they were brought up in good habits, despite their mother's failings.

This Towneley-worship fitted Butler's philosophy. Nor was his ideal much amiss : he merely failed to present it plausibly, as most men do when they set themselves to depict perfection. How could it be otherwise, when it is in the very nature of ideals not to be attainable ? Butler knew well enough, in his sober moments, that the Towneleys of his imagination neither did, nor ever would, exist. He made a much better hand at describing what he meant in *Erewhon Revisited,* when he brought Mr. Higgs—the

Sunchild—that is, himself—face to face with George, his son by Yram. For George did not have to be dressed up as a Victorian gentleman, and could be made to appear like a young god without any clash with circumstance. For Butler, George and Towneley were one and the same person : for his readers they are as different as chalk from cheese.

Yet both, by their qualities of unconscious bravery, bring out Butler's timidity. Festing Jones, in his *Life*, preferred to call it " sensitiveness " ; and that of course, among other things, it was. Butler had too little personal bravery for his ideas to shelter behind in comfort. Satirists, I think, often have. They yelp at the world, because they find it uncomfortable ; but they do not like it when the world hits back. And they are apt to fancy that the world is hitting back at them when it is not thinking about them at all. Indeed, that it should not be thinking about them is the unkindest cut ; for surely it ought to be thinking how right, after all, they are. Butler's ideal world was peopled with magnanimous heroes, who were above either being hit or hitting back. Meanwhile, he wanted a world in which timid people could live without being terrorised—above all by their parents while they were young.

CHAPTER III

PARENTS AND CHILDREN

THE normal relations between parents and children have changed greatly since Butler wrote *The Way of All Flesh*—and still more since the period in which the earlier scenes of the story were cast. They have indeed changed so thoroughly that it is no longer easy to recapture in full the spirit of the relations which he attacked. That the picture given in the novel was taken, with some variations, largely from his own experience of boyhood and youth no one has ever disputed ; but the truth of the picture has been called into question, in its application to Butler's own life. There is a book, written by someone who knew the family well,[1] in which Canon Butler appears as a charming, bene-volent old gentleman, who clearly would not have hurt a fly, much less played the tyrant over his son and done his best to thwart him and to ruin his career. Correspondingly, Samuel's reactions to his upbringing are made to seem the products of a perverse and morbid imagination. Canon Butler, we are given to understand, was not at all the sort of person his son made him out to be in *The Way of All Flesh*— that is, if we are to take the Reverend Theobald Pontifex as having been meant as a portrait of Butler's father.

There are, it must be borne in mind, two " heavy fathers " in Butler's novel—old Pontifex, Theobald's father, and Theobald himself. This was essential to Butler's conception ;

[1] *Samuel Butler and His Family Relations*, by Mrs. R. S. Garnett. (Dent, 1926.)

for he wanted to show how Theobald's behaviour towards his children had been influenced by the parental treatment that he had received in his own youth. Certain touches in the behaviour of old George Pontifex towards Theobald—especially in connection with Theobald's objections to being ordained—we know to have been taken from Canon Butler's treatment of Samuel on a similar occasion—when Samuel, unlike Theobald in the story—stuck out and got his own way. But George Pontifex, the publisher, was clearly not intended to be a portrait of Canon Butler. As far as he was taken from anybody, he was meant to be taken from Butler's grandfather, the headmaster and bishop, whose biography Samuel was later to write, partly by way of amends, when he had found out how wrong he had been about Bishop Butler's character. We know that one of his reasons for wishing to rewrite the early chapters of *The Way of All Flesh* was that he had it in mind to do his grandfather better justice ; and we may be thankful that he never did, for he would almost certainly have spoilt the book. We must take old George Pontifex, not as either Bishop Butler or Canon Butler, but as an imaginary portrait of the strong-minded, obstinate, wilful, openly tyrannical parent of the old school, of whom Theobald—the Canon Butler of his son's imagining—was but a pale and fundamentally weak-minded reflection. Butler's point is that Theobald, naturally weak, felt he ought to behave as his own father had behaved to him, and did so behave as far as it was in him to do so, playing the weak tyrant with effects fully as devastating as the robuster tyranny of the older generation could have brought about—indeed, perhaps more devastating, for the roaring kind of domestic tyrant is not usually the worst.

But was Theobald Pontifex meant to be a fair portrait of

Butler's father? If we had only the novel itself and Mrs. Garnett's account of Thomas Butler to go by, it would be just possible to argue that Theobald was never meant to bear any close resemblance to the Canon, and that he was as much an imaginary person as George Pontifex. This view, however, is entirely irreconcilable with what Butler wrote in his letters to Miss Savage both about Theobald and about his father. There is no shadow of doubt that Butler did regard his father as having treated him thoroughly badly, as having tried to keep him in subjection from childhood onwards, as having done his best to thwart and cross him on every occasion, and as having been, to use his own words, his " worst enemy." Butler never suggested that his father was aware of behaving in this way : on the contrary, he accepted the fact that Canon Butler supposed himself to be acting for his son's good and from a sense of duty. That, however, did not at all mend matters ; and enough of the facts are undisputed to make it clear that Canon Butler was addicted to what his son called " will-shaking " and to the use of his money-power as a means of attempting to bring him to heel whenever he tried to go his own way. Nor is there any doubt that Canon Butler did, on the occasion of Samuel's refusal to be ordained, write to his son much in the terms in which George Pontifex is made to write to Theobald in the novel—that is, with a complete contempt for his scruples and with a threat to cut him off completely unless he gave way. Nor do such of Canon Butler's letters as have survived convey a more agreeable impression of his parental manners.

What, then, are we to make of the contrast between Samuel Butler's and Mrs. Garnett's pictures of the Canon? I think the conclusion must be that there is, despite appearances, no real conflict between the portraits, but only between the painters of them and between their several experiences. It is, or was, perfectly possible for a man to be at one and the same time a benevolent and amiable person in all the outward relations of life and an irritable husband and father. It is perfectly possible for a father to present every appearance of loving his son, and indeed to feel sure that he does love him, and yet to be continually at loggerheads with him in private life. It is perfectly possible for a man, and especially for a clergyman, to appear both to others and to himself to be actuated by the highest moral principles and the most kindly sentiments, and yet to be domestically an oppressor, mistaking his own preferences and predilections for the will of God, and his own impulse to exact unquestioning obedience for the voice of duty. Samuel Butler was half-wrong in thinking that his father never liked him, and quite wrong if he thought that his father in any way meant to be his enemy. But he was half-right too, about the disliking ; for Canon Butler evidently found children a nuisance, and the son's ways from childhood evidently cut right across the father's conceptions of right and wrong, and of the dutifulness to be expected of children. Samuel combined with his timidity an enquiring spirit and a keen sense of justice—both to others and to himself. His father, on the other hand, was clearly of the mind that it was best to ask as few questions as possible, and cared little for justice and much for the conventional morality which often leads to flouting it. He had fully convinced himself that this morality was the code for men to live by, and the only passport to salvation ; and if his son thought differently, so much the worse for his son.

There was, then, an incompatibility of temperament that made itself apparent from the first moment when Samuel

Butler began to think for himself; and we can take it for granted that he began young. Samuel's sense of justice was again and again outraged, as he makes plain in the story. The episode that turns on Theobald's treating Ernest's saying "Tum" when he meant "Come" as a serious crime is almost certainly taken from life; and the reader will recall other instances. Besides this, Samuel obviously became aware very early that his father, instead of giving him straight answers to his questions, often put him off; and there grew up in his mind a conception of his father as an unkind, unjust, unaccountable power that continually thwarted or disappointed him without giving him any of the reasons why. Undoubtedly, this view of his father grew with him into an obsession that never left him as long as Canon Butler was alive, though he was able to feel somewhat less unkindly when he had come into his property and was completely independent of the financial whip. This conception of his father led him to conclude, wrongly, that Canon Butler had no affection for him. He kept saying that he would have been ready, as a boy, to love his father if he had been given half a chance, but that his father's attitude seemed always to be one of dislike. Dislike, however, or at least half-dislike, is not incompatible with affection; and I think there can be no doubt that Canon Butler, while he regarded his children as a very great nuisance, after a fashion loved them, or at any rate supposed he did.

If love there was, it was strongly mixed with disapproval; for the Canon was narrow-minded, and Butler's tastes and questionings frightened him. In his fright he attempted to drive out by force those of his son's qualities that he disliked; and in doing this he gave Samuel the impression of a severity wholly untempered by affection. Butler felt that his father had done his best to knock clean out of him everything that was most characteristically his own, and had thus turned him from a naturally joyous person, with an ardent will to live and to be happy, into a crabbed and unhappy rebel, always expecting to be snubbed and put down. To a great extent, this is what did happen ; and the mark of it stayed on Butler to the end of his life. Whether we blame Canon Butler much or little, it is beyond doubt that his influence on his son was thoroughly bad. Butler's attitude to his father was one of morbid obsession ; and that it was so must, one feels, have been at any rate in part the father's fault.

Towards his mother Butler felt quite differently. The portrait of Christina in *The Way of All Flesh* is that of a thoroughly silly woman. But it is never that of a nasty woman ; and it is entirely free from resentment, though he represents her throughout as Theobald's aider and abetter even in his worst moments and strips her naked with a callousness that would have been impossible unless he had been very badly hurt in youth. Butler knew that his mother loved him ; but he was also well aware that she loved his father infinitely more and would, as he said of Christina, have gladly chopped him, or anyone else in the world, into little pieces if it had been necessary for her husband's convenience. Christina, in the story, always took sides in the last resort against the children in any affair in which Theobald was involved and was addicted to the sharpest of practices in getting them to confess their sins and then betraying them. This is probably an exaggerated version of Mrs. Butler's actual behaviour, while her children were young ; and there is evidence that it was not the whole story. She seems to have mediated with success on Samuel's behalf in the dispute that followed his refusal of ordination, and to have persuaded her husband to let him have the capital for his New Zealand venture, instead of cutting him off.

For, when it became clear that no threats would make Samuel Butler into a clergyman, there arose the question of what was to be done with him instead. In Canon Butler's view, there were only two possible professions for a son of his who was so misguided as to reject the Church as a calling. He could become either a schoolmaster or a lawyer ; but Samuel regarded these two careers with almost as much abhorrence as ordination. He wrote to his mother " I would migrate, learn to farm in England, turn homoeopathic doctor, or learn to paint, in which last I have strong reason to believe I should succeed." [He was already taking lessons in drawing.] " But ' No ' from my father. To the other two courses, namely the law or a schoolmaster's life, I say ' No ' no less decidedly. You would, with the best intentions in the world, make me a bed that I know very well would not fit me. I know that when I am in, escape is impossible ; and, knowing that I have duties to myself to perform even more binding on me than those to my parents, with all respect adopt the alternative of rejecting the pounds, shillings, and pence and going in search of my own bread my own way." [1]

This letter was written when, after some months experience of work in a London slum parish—work which he afterwards turned to account in *The Way of All Flesh*—Samuel Butler had finally refused ordination and his father had been brought round to the discussion of alternatives. The Canon, it will be observed, was now offering financial

[1] Butler to his Mother. Quoted from H. Festing Jones's *Life*, Vol. I, p. 65. Written from Cambridge, May 10, 1859.

help if his son would take to schoolmastering or to the law, but on no other condition, and Butler was answering that he would sooner forfeit the help and live by his wits in his own way. Already he was thinking seriously of becoming a painter ; but this roused the strongest opposition at home, on the ground that painting was not respectable and artists were known to be an immoral lot. The dispute ended with Canon Butler coming round to the notion of emigration as the least evil course left open, and arranging to plant his errant son in a colony—that of Canterbury in New Zealand —which had at any rate the merit of having been established on sound Church of England principles.

To Canterbury, then, Samuel Butler went, with capital supplied and more promised by his father, to settle down as a sheep-farmer. The Canon, indeed, seems at this stage to have behaved generously, in a financial sense, though he had qualms later on—probably out of fear that the money would be lost—and sent out in the end less than he had promised. In this way he earned, instead of his son's gratitude, another black mark ; for Butler had entered into engagements on the strength of his father's promise, and resented the failure to keep it.

That trouble, however, came only later ; and for the time being Canon Butler seems to have been behaving in a way that belies his son's account of him. Nor does the next episode in their relations look as if the Canon was so set against his son, or so determined to thwart him, as Butler was accustomed to make out. Had this been really the state of affairs, is it conceivable that Canon Butler would have been at the pains of making a book out of his son's letters home from New Zealand, of seeking out a publisher for them, and thus of giving his son his first impetus towards a literary career ? Samuel Butler always maintained later on that his father had spoilt his letters in editing them, cutting out the best bits, and turning what he had written into a dull and commonplace book. Very likely the Canon did prune the letters of some of their most characteristic passages ; but it does not follow that he was actuated even by unconscious malice. It seems much more likely that, being a very shockable person, he was simply shocked by some of his son's outspokennesses and removed them because they seemed to him to mar a work of which in general he thought well. If he had not admired Samuel's letters and been pleased at his son's demonstration of literary talent, he would never have set about making a book out of them at all. Nor did he in fact make a dull book : on the contrary, *A First Year in Canterbury Settlement*, though there is nothing very special about it, is a readable little volume, and shows an excellent talent for description of men and things. Samuel Butler, one cannot help feeling, disliked it because he associated it with his father, much more than on account of any intrinsic defects, or even of the loss of some of the bits he valued most. It is galling, of course, to have one's favourite passages cut out ; but more than this is needed to explain Butler's attitude. Nor can I help thinking it significant that a man as tenacious of memory as Butler was never seems to have told even Miss Savage, to whom he confided the information that his father had spoilt the book, what even one of the lost jewels of his first volume had been.[1]

At all events, Butler disliked his father, and strongly disapproved of the way he had been brought up. He was in

---

[1] In all Butler's later books, there is a strong element of *gaminerie*—of sheer grinning naughtiness. There is none of this in *A First Year*. Probably his father cut it out. Canon Butler liked a joke, but preferred it mild to bitter.

effect assailing, in the person of his own father, the entire race of fathers who conceived themselves entitled not merely to the unquestioning obedience of their children, but also to shake their wills at them, to threaten to cut them off with a shilling on the occasion of any "disobedience," and to indoctrinate them with the parental ideas, without allowing to them, more than was unavoidable, any opportunity of independent judgment. The child, according to this once common view, had to be brought up in the way of righteousness—, that is, as the parents believed it to be—and this had to be done by a severity which stamped, promptly and without compunction, on any sign of "self-will." Man's natural unrighteousness was the assumption that underlay this code of parental discipline. The child's "self-will" was regarded, not as the growth of personality, but as the manifestation of original sin ; and virtue was looked upon not as the natural outcome of a good disposition but as the artificial product of parental inflexibility. Some shadow of this abominable doctrine lingered on into my own childhood. My own parents, I am happy to say, never practised it on me ; but I was well aware, even as a child, both that their tastes were not mine and that they were sometimes blaming themselves for being unable to bring themselves to try knocking the nonsense out of me, and were entertaining fears that their leniency might do me harm. Moreover, I occasionally encountered other parents who did attempt to live up to the old rule and were perpetually roaring at their children and badgering them about ; and I grew up conscious of being a beneficiary of the change in parental manners, and with enough knowledge of the discarded rules of parental conduct to appreciate the reality of what Butler was driving at when, as a very young man, I first read his books.

Butler's grudge against his father was, I think, at bottom a grudge at never being encouraged or allowed, as far as parental influence could prevent him, either to follow his natural bent or to think things out fairly and objectively for himself. He felt this the more strongly because Canon Butler simply took it for granted from his schooldays, if not from his very infancy, that he was to become a parson, without any attempt either to measure his fitness for the priestly calling or to give him any chance of weighing up the evidence for and against those things in which parsons are supposed to profess belief. The Canon himself was clearly not of a speculative temper, and had never been visited by any religious doubts, or had forgotten all about them, if they had never existed—though he may, like Theobald in the novel, have doubted, for all I know, whether he had a vocation to the priesthood and have shrunk back when his time came for being ordained. If so, he had, like Theobald, settled down very thoroughly to the life of a country clergyman, and felt no qualms about sending his son, with no questions asked, into the same vocation. He had all the assurance of the timid that questions are dangerous and trodden paths best ; and he took it so much for granted that any son of his ought to become a clergyman as never to consider whether his actual son was fitted for his intended calling. Samuel, on the other hand, seems to have been always asking questions to which he expected reasoned answers ; and though it did not for a long time ever occur to him that he could evade the destiny that had been marked out for him, when the question had once raised itself in his mind it kept on coming back. Curiously enough, during his undergraduate years at Cambridge he seems to have given the problem hardly any thought. He explained this

later by the state of the University at the time of his residence.
" When I was at Cambridge the Evangelical movement had
become a matter of ancient history ; Tractarianism had spent
its force and had subsided into a nine days' wonder ; *The
Vestiges of Creation* had long since ceased to be talked about ;
the Catholic aggression scare had lost its terrors ; Ritualism
was still unnoticed by the general public ; the Gorham and
Hampden controversies were hull-down beneath Time's
horizon ; Dissent was not spreading ; the Crimean War
was the engrossing subject in men's thoughts, and there was
no enemy to the faith which could secure even a languid
interest ; at no time, probably, in the century, could an
ordinary observer have detected less sign of coming disturbance than at the date of which I am writing." [1]

Thus it was that the sole evidence of Butler's having
thought at all about religious matters during his undergraduate years is the best evidence of his not having thought
about them in any serious sense.   There existed in his day
at Cambridge the very Low Church group of religious
enthusiasts known as " Simeonites "—after Charles Simeon
the evangelical preacher.   Simeon's followers in Cambridge
were mostly very poor men reading for ordination ; and
in *The Way of All Flesh* we get an account of their uncouth
manners and aggressive pieties.   Ernest Pontifex, in the
story, looked down on them as no gentlemen and joined in
making a mock of them ; and so did Butler himself, in his
undergraduate days.   Butler indeed wrote a lampoon upon
them, in the form of a mock Simeonite tract, which has
been preserved and is not in good taste.   In the story he
makes Ernest, when after taking his degree he began to

[1] From *A Clergyman's Doubts,* published in *The Examiner,* February 15,
1879.

think seriously about ordination, attend a Simeonite preaching and fall under the preacher's spell ; and almost certainly the experience was his own. It belongs, however, to the period after he had taken his degree. As an undergraduate, he merely mocked ; and the proof that he was not thinking seriously about religion is that, in so mocking, he does not appear to have been led to think at all about his own intention to let himself be made a parson. His mind was not on the issue at all, until he was brought face to face with ordination as an immediate and irrevocable step that he was expected to take.

Butler took his degree at Cambridge in 1858, the year before *The Origin of Species* was published. His " doubts " began when, having taken the Classical Tripos, he began to prepare seriously for ordination, and his reluctance to become a parson was greatly strengthened by a few months of parish work in a slum area in the West End of London, undertaken as part of this preparation. From his experiences during these months he drew his account of Ernest Pontifex's life in Ashpit Place and, in all probability, his satirical picture of Pryer, the High Church curate, with his utterly disingenuous ritualism and his plans for a " College of Spiritual Pathology " —though Pryer's speculative excesses with Ernest's money came, not from this period, but from his later associations with Henry Hoare, the banker. It was during this period of preparation for the ministry that he began to study Christian evidences for himself and that " doubts " began seriously to afflict him ; but even then he was slow to admit his " unbelief" in major things, and merely became more and more convinced of his unsuitableness for the life of a parson. His letters show that, even when he had reached the point of definitely refusing to be ordained, he was still

4

not at all sure how deep his " doubts " went : nor did he
become sure until he had worried the whole problem out
for himself in the quietude of his upland sheep-run in New
Zealand.

Long, however, before he had reached any clear assurance
about his religious convictions he had become quite certain
that he did not want to be a clergyman : that he would
not be a clergyman ; and that his father had taken an
unwarrantable liberty in trying to make a clergyman of
him without giving him a fair opportunity of understanding
the " cons " as well as the " pros." If, as he saw was the
case, his father was quite unaware of the existence of any
" cons," that was in his eyes no excuse. His father ought
to have been aware of the " cons " : he ought to have been
prepared, as an advocate of Christianity, fairly and squarely
to meet the arguments against belief in it, and he ought in
common fairness to have put these arguments in his son's
way before allowing him to commit himself irrevocably to
a career in which he would be pledged to take one particular
side. No doubt, this line of attack on his father's attitude
became explicit only by degrees in Samuel Butler's mind ;
but long before he could have put his case thus plainly he
was in revolt against the parental requirement of unreasoning
obedience in thought as well as in deed.

All the rest of his life, Butler never forgot the narrow
escape he had achieved from being made into a clergyman.
Ministers of religion, he always contended, were to be
regarded as paid advocates, who got their living by preaching
certain doctrines, and were accordingly the very last persons
to be accepted as impartial witnesses to the truth of what
they preached. Especially if they were married and had
families, and were without private means, their line of

retreat was cut off, and they simply had to go on believing, after a fashion, because the consequences of acknowledged unbelief would have been so very unpleasant. He thought he saw ample evidence of this attitude of unreal belief in the clergymen he met with, and in the writings of the most acclaimed expositors of Christian doctrines. When he set himself to read the works of the best-known Bible commentators, he was shocked by their tone; for instead of straight, objective arguments based on the rigorous use of reasoning power, he found in them only apologetics. Difficulties, such as the plain discrepancies between the accounts given by the four Evangelists of Christ's life, death and resurrection, he found met neither with effective reconciliations of the discrepant narratives nor with admissions that reconciliation was impossible, but instead with appeals to faith, as against reason, as the final court of appeal. Faith, these commentators told him, was the key to the right understanding of the Gospel story; but he was totally unable to see how faith could legitimately be invoked against reason, or could, by any rational person, be twisted into a means of enabling men to believe in inconsistent things.

Mixed up with Butler's resentment against his father for trying to make him into a clergyman against his will was a second resentment centring upon his father's attitude about money. Thomas Butler was well-to-do, and had every prospect of being rich when he came into a large property to which he, and his children after him, had a legal reversion. It seems clear that he was prepared to behave open-handedly towards his son in the matter of settling him comfortably in the Church; but when Butler refused to be ordained his father's immediate reaction was to say that he should not have a penny. Butler, in his letters home, did not openly deny his father's right to take this line, provided that he was allowed to go his own way; but he undoubtedly resented his father's attitude, not only because he regarded it as unkind and unjust in itself, but also because he felt that he had a moral, if not a legal, right to enjoy at once some of the money that was due by law to become his on his father's death. He accordingly felt that his father was being doubly unjust as well as unkind; and this feeling went a long way towards strengthening his views about the proper relations between parents and children. The children, in his view, were the parents continuing their lives, and had fully as good a right as the parents to benefit by the family property. This view of Butler's doubtless became fully articulate only later; but the germ of it was plainly there in his feeling about his father when he was threatened with being cut off for refusing to take what would have been, for him, the immoral step of being ordained.

Angered as Canon Butler was by his son's refusal to be ordained, there was, as we have seen, no final breach between them on that account. Indeed, the Canon sent his son off well supplied with money, and they were probably on better terms during the first year or two of Butler's residence in New Zealand than at any other time in their lives. The gulf, however, had been opened up again before Butler came back—by his father's failure to let him have some additional capital which he had promised in a generous mood; and it seems pretty clear that Butler's return, with enough money realised by the sale of his sheep and run to make him modestly independent, was not relished. Canon Butler had advanced capital in order to enable his son to establish himself as a sheep-farmer—not in order that he might sell out at a profit after five years abroad and use the augmented capital to become an artist, the very career which his father had most emphatically rejected for him before he went away. This however, was precisely what Butler, on his return from New Zealand in 1864, proceeded to do, in the confidence that he would be able to do it without needing any further help from his father—though, no doubt, help would have been welcomed if it had been given without unacceptable conditions.

It needs to be borne in mind, for the understanding of Samuel Butler's attitude, that Canon Butler was a wealthy man, with every prospect of becoming, by a known reversion, wealthier still. We have seen that Samuel Butler, on account of his expectation of coming into property, by legal right under the reversion, on his father's death, felt that he had a right to expect his father to help him liberally with capital during his life, whereas Canon Butler probably felt that his son was in effect cheating by applying the money he had been given to a purpose for which it had not been meant. If, after his return, Butler had been able to live quietly on his money, and had not needed to make any further appeals to his father, very likely the Canon would in due course have given him more. There were, however, two reasons why this did not happen. The first was Charles Pauli, the very handsome but impecunious barrister with whom Butler had made friends in New Zealand. Pauli was ill, and was most anxious to return to England. He said he would die if he had to stay in New Zealand. He wanted only the means of support for a few years while he established himself as a barrister in England, and his life would be saved and his fortune made. Butler, for his part, had developed a romantic attachment to Pauli ; and his infatuation went to the length of a promise to allow him a regular income until

he had been able to establish his position at the bar. This
act of romantic friendship cost Butler dear : Pauli continued
to be a drain on him for most of his life, and went on drawing
his allowance long after he could well have done without it.
He concealed his circumstances from his benefactor, and
before long ceased even to pretend to be fond of him. But
Butler, even when he knew that Pauli was treating him
badly, went on paying whenever it was at all within his
power, to the extent of eating up the last of his capital in
order to help his friend. The story of Butler and Pauli is
a very strange story, to which we shall come back.[1] It is
relevant here only because Pauli was one of the two things
that threw all Butler's plans out of gear.

The other thing was the loss of most of his capital in
imprudent speculation, into which he was led by his friend
Henry Hoare, a member of the famous banking house.
Hoare, in a series of wild company promoting activities,
ruined himself as well as most of his friends. For Butler the
disaster was severe. It occurred in 1874, and for the next
five years he and Pauli were living on what was left of his
capital and on a legacy which came to him on his mother's
death in 1873. By 1879 there was nothing left, and he had
to go to his father for help. Canon Butler, after a good deal
of acrimonious discussion, which confirmed his son's views
about his character, agreed to allow him £300 a year, but
only on condition that he stopped financing Pauli. At that
stage, Canon Butler refused to allow his son to anticipate
his interest in the reversion already mentioned, which would
have made him comfortably off ; and this added to Butler's
annoyance. But two years later, for reasons connected with
Samuel's brother Tom, the Canon changed his mind. Butler

[1] See page 101.

got the capital due to him under the reversion, and his more pressing financial difficulties came to an end. He celebrated his freedom by resuming the allowance to Pauli, which he had been forced to suspend two years before.

Butler's financial difficulties left him with a great horror of speculation and a passion for secure investments. He made use of the lesson he had learnt in *The Way of All Flesh*, by making Pryer speculate with Ernest Pontifex's money and lose it all. To his speculative adventures was due his residence in Canada, to which we owe his best-known essay in verse—the *Psalm of Montreal*. What concerns us here is the effect which his financial troubles had on his relations with his father. These two were usually at their worst when money was at issue. Canon Butler thought any financial help entitled him not only to attach conditions, but also to play the inquisitor without limit into his son's affairs ; whereas Samuel held that his father ought to let him have when he needed it most money which was due to come to him in any event later on, when he might need it much less, or not at all. Their standpoints were never modified, and every time they discussed money their tempers were sadly frayed.

Butler's money troubles had another effect on him : they made him ashamed. He approved of successful, untroubled people ; and he saw that the possession of safely invested capital was one of the principal conditions of the kind of happiness he wanted for himself. In revolt as he was against many aspects of the Victorian gospel, he was thoroughly at one with that unspoken article of the Victorian creed which laid down that lack of money is the root of most, if not of all, evil. Love of money became for him, in his days of adversity, one of the cardinal virtues. He was very ready

to proclaim that hardly shall a poor man enter into the
Kingdom of Heaven. He was piqued that his books did
not sell quite as much because his failure to make money
by them was a blow to his self-respect as because he wanted
literary recognition. And yet he knew all the time that the
very last thing he wanted to do was to write books in order
to sell them. It was contrary to his self-respect to try to
give the public what it wanted ; but it was also contrary to
his self-respect that the public should not want what he
wanted to write.

There was a similar tangle in many of Samuel Butler's
affairs—not least in his relations with his father. Given
Canon Butler's standards, Samuel was an impossible son :
given Samuel's, the Canon was an impossible father. Yet,
however much they quarrelled and however hard things
they said and thought of each other, they never came to a
decisive rupture. Canon Butler never cut off his son ; and
Samuel never left off going to stay at home, attending family
prayers, and corresponding on outwardly amicable terms
with both his parents, while they were alive, and with his
sisters. The more violently he wrote about them all to
Miss Savage, of whose sympathy he could feel sure, the less
did it seem possible for him to break with them. Butler
had, in fact, deep down in him, a strong sense of family
solidarity. Even though he made Ernest Pontifex say, in
The Way of All Flesh, that " the family is a survival of the
principle which is more logically embodied in the compound
animal—and the compound animal is a form of life which
has been found incompatible with high development," and
urge that it should be confined as an institution " to the
lower and less progressive races," he remained personally
under its spell. Nor did he really wish to abolish the family,

even among the higher races : he wished to reform it by
teaching fathers and mothers to exercise more common sense.
There is a passage in *The Way of All Flesh* in which Overton,
the narrator, who is one of the incarnations of Butler himself, is describing to Ernest how Theobald Pontifex ought to
have behaved to him.

> " It was not much that was wanted. To make no mysteries
> where Nature has made none, to bring his conscience under
> something like reasonable control, to give Ernest his head a
> little more, to ask fewer questions, and to give him pocket
> money with a desire that it should be spent upon *menus
> plaisirs.* . . ."
> " ' Call that not much indeed,' laughed Ernest. . . . ' Why,
> it is the whole duty of a father.' "

And then he makes Ernest add that " it is the mystery-
making that is the worst evil," and that " if people would
dare to speak to one another unreservedly, there would be
a good deal less sorrow in the world a hundred years hence."
Butler's positive idea of what a good father ought to be
like can be studied in *Erewhon Revisited,* where he made
Yram's husband a representation of his ideal. He wanted
fathers to be, above all else, frank, open, and easygoing ;
and, whatever Canon Butler's virtues may have been, it
was not in his nature to be frank or easygoing with the
ugly duckling that had found its way into his nest.

Mrs. Garnett, in the book already mentioned, says that
she finds Butler's picture of Ernest's sister, Charlotte Pontifex,
in *The Way of All Flesh,* more perplexing even than his
pictures of Theobald and Christina, and refuses altogether
to accept it as bearing any resemblance to either of the Miss
Butler's. It is, however, plainly on the evidence, a composite
picture, drawn mainly from Harriet Butler, who became

Mrs. Bridges and, early widowed, returned to the family home, and only to the extent of a few stylistic touches from his younger sister, May. Of May, it is clear that he was after a fashion fond, though in his letters to Miss Savage he made frequent mock of her epistolary style. Of Harriet he was quite clearly not fond at all, and Charlotte Pontifex is mainly Harriet, but, as far as one can judge, a Harriet softened rather than exaggerated. On Mrs. Garnett's own showing, Harriet Butler must have been a dreadful person ; and it is evident that she, out of religious bigotry, took a leading part in stiffening her parents against her " infidel " brother. She appears to have pursued him with relentless disapproval, even to the extent, on the occasion of his last illness in Italy, of refusing to let her nephew, who was there in a yacht of his own and could have brought the invalid home, hear of his plight, for fear his soul might be imperilled by contact with a blasphemer. One cannot help feeling that Harriet may have been responsible for a good deal of Butler's bitterness towards his father, by acerbating quarrels which, but for her attitude, might have been set aside as both men mellowed. It was Harriet who made Samuel's visits home really difficult ; but even Harriet's presence could not induce him to stay away. Mrs Garnett maintains that Harriet was not odious, despite her determined bigotry : nevertheless she has managed to paint of her a portrait nearly as unpleasant as Butler's account of Charlotte in *The Way of All Flesh*.

In reckoning up Butler's indictment of Victorian family life we must never lose sight of the fact that his description is of a *clerical* household. He stresses this point himself. After saying that " it is a matter of common observation in England that the sons of clergymen are frequently unsatisfactory," he goes on to give the explanation as he sees it.

> " The clergyman is expected to be a kind of human Sunday . . . He is paid for this business of leading a stricter life than other people. It is his *raison d'être*. If his parishioners feel that he does this, they approve of him, for they look upon him as their own contribution towards what they deem a holy life. . . . But his home is his castle as much as that of any other Englishman, and with him, as with others, unnatural tension in public is followed by exhaustion when tension is no longer necessary. His children are the most defenceless things he can reach, and it is on them in nine cases out of ten that he will relieve his mind."

Then Butler goes on to say that the clergyman, being a paid advocate whose living depends on holding a particular set of views, can never afford to be frank, either with his children or with anyone else. He says of Theobald and Christina that " when they came to Battersby [Theobald's parish] they had every desire to fulfil the duties of their position, and to devote themselves to the honour and glory of God " ; and then he adds " But it was Theobald's duty to see the honour and glory of God through the eyes of a Church which had lived three hundred years without finding reason to change a single one of its opinions."

> " In the course of time," Butler comments, " he and his wife became persuaded even to unconsciousness [an essentially Butlerian touch] that no one could even dwell under their roof without deep cause for thankfulness. Their children, their servants, their parishioners must be fortunate *ipso facto* that they were theirs. There was no road to happiness here or hereafter, but the road that they had themselves travelled, no good people who did not think as they did upon every subject, and no reasonable person who had wants the gratification of which would be inconvenient to them—Theobald and Christina."

Then Butler sums up.

> " This was how it came to pass that their children were white
> and puny : they were suffering from *home-sickness*. They were
> starving, through being over-crammed with the wrong things.
> Nature came down upon them, but she did not come down
> on Theobald and Christina. Why should she ? They were
> not leading a starved existence. There are two classes of persons
> in this world, those who sin, and those who are sinned against ;
> if a man must belong to either, he had better belong to the
> first than to the second."

This reads bitter, and was probably written when Butler
was pinched for money and was feeling his bitterness against
his father for keeping him so. To the extent of its truth, it
could be applied to other households besides those of clergymen ; but Butler was right in regarding the clerical household as subject to special trials and temptations. The " human
Sunday," unless he has a peculiarly sweet temper, must take
it out of somebody. It may be his wife, or his children, or
both. If his wife humours him and believes in him to the
*n*th, perhaps his children are all the more likely to get it in
the neck when he is feeling the strain. At all events probably
they were so in the Victorian age, when fathers could lose
their tempers with their children in a glow of righteousness,
and could assure themselves without prick of conscience that
it was all for the children's good.

CHAPTER IV

THE FAIR HAVEN

RELIGION and its place in everyday life, and the conflict between religion and science, played a big part in the development of Samuel Butler's mind. From the moment when he did begin to think seriously about what was involved in being ordained he was perpetually worrying his head about religion until he had settled firmly where he stood about it, in a positive as well as in a merely negative sense. Then, having disposed of the entire problem to his own satisfaction, he ceased, like Ernest Pontifex, to trouble himself any more about it, and directed his logical faculties and his detective instinct away from the "higher criticism" to such other issues as the authorship of the *Odyssey* and the geography of the Homeric poems, the true inwardness of Shakespeare's *Sonnets*, and the rescue of the memory of Tabachetti and other forgotten painters. The faculties which he applied in these later studies were much the same as he had used in his "religious" period—a refusal to take anything at all on trust from the people who were supposed to know, and indeed a preconception that they were probably all wrong, a love of inverting current beliefs (the same love as made him delight in turning familiar proverbs inside out), and a readiness to be totally captured by an idea, in such a way that it took full possession of him and went buzzing round and round in his head until he had relieved himself of it by the expulsive force of literary creation.

Butler wrote nothing on religion or scientific issues between his articles on *The Deadlock in Darwinism* in 1890 and *Erewhon Revisited* in 1900–1901. Then, in his sequel to *Erewhon,* he went back to the central theme of *The Fair Haven* and, in his account of the growth of the " Sunchild Legend," restated his theory of the development of the Christian mythology about Christ's ascension into heaven. *Erewhon Revisited* is in effect a rewriting of part of *The Fair Haven* in Erewhonian terms ; but the writing of it did not mean that Butler had any new notions to spring upon the world, or that there had been any revival of his interest in matters of religion. He had often before considered producing a sequel to his one popular success, which he revised and partly rewrote in connection with it. I rather think he wrote it because he had nothing fresh that was occupying his mind at the moment, and therefore reverted to an old idea. Certainly the theme he took for it did not indicate any re-opening of the religious question in his own mind.

Butler, when he had lost his faith in orthodox Christianity, and had discarded all belief in its miraculous element, remained a Theist, in the sense that he was sure the whole universe was animated by a presence to which he gave the name of " God." He set down in his *Note-books* that " Thought pure and simple is as near to God as we can get ; it is through this that we are linked with God." And again, here is a selection of sayings about God from the *Note-books* that will serve as well as any summary to indicate Butler's general position :

> " Those who say there is a God are wrong unless they mean at the same time that there is no God, and vice versa. The difference is the same as that between plus nothing and minus nothing, and it is hard to say which we ought to admire and

thank most—the first theist or the first atheist. Nevertheless, for many reasons, the plus nothing is to be preferred."

" God is the unknown, and hence the nothing *qua* us. He is also the ensemble of all we know, and hence the everything *qua* us. So that the most absolute nothing and the most absolute everything are extremes that meet (like all other extremes) in God."

" As long as there is an unknown there will be a God for all practical purposes."

" To know God better is only to realise more fully how impossible it is that we should ever know him at all. I cannot tell which is the more childish—to deny him, or to attempt to define him."

" Presently, instead of seeing life as a thing created by God, we shall see God and life as one thing, there being no life without God nor God without life, where there is life there is God and where there is God there is life."

" There is lots of God and lots of flesh, but the flesh has always got too much God or too little, and the God has always too little flesh or too much."

" God is not so white as he is painted, and he gets on better with the Devil than people think."

" The fight between them [theist and atheist] is as to whether God should be called God or should have some other name."

" Everything that catches on to realism and naturalism as much as Christianity does must be affected by any professed modification in our views of realism and naturalism."

" I do not know or care whether the expression ' God ' has scientific accuracy or no, nor yet whether it has theological value ; I know nothing either of the one or the other, beyond looking upon the recognised exponents both of science and theology with equal distrust ; but, for convenience, I am sure that there is nothing like it—I mean for convenience of getting quickly at the right or wrong of a matter. While you are fumbling away with your political economy or your biblical precepts to know whether you shall let old Mrs. So-and-so have 5s. or no, another, who has just asked himself which would be most well-pleasing in the sight of God, will be told in a moment that he should give her—or not give her—the 5s. As a general rule she had better have the 5s. at once, but sometimes we must give God to understand that, though we should be very glad to do what he would have of us if we reasonably could, yet the present is one of those occasions on which we must decline to do so."

" Whether it is right to say that one believes in God and Christianity without intending what one knows the hearer intends one to intend depends on how much or how little the hearer can understand. Life is not an exact science, it is an art."

Such was Butler's " theology," and it amounted to a sort of Pantheism. It was closely connected with his view of human personality, which in turn was linked to his doctrine about inherited memory. This doctrine was, indeed, to his mind the key to the whole problem. He considered personality to be continuous between parents and children, and in effect between all living things—for he regarded them all as parts of a developing and leavening universal stuff. This stuff was God, or at any rate all that was fine and healthily growing in it was God. Atheism was right, in the sense that there was no personal God apart from this thought-stuff of the universe : theism was right, in the sense that this stuff was divine. Butler had a profound respect for the religious sentiment whenever he could find it divorced from mumbo-jumbo,[1] and a profound disrespect for every scientific theory

He once said that he would join the Catholic Church, if only it would agree to cut out all the supernatural elements of its doctrine.

that seemed to him to dethrone the mind-stuff that was his idea of God. Out of this arose his search for a theory of evolution that should give mind, or will, or "trying," the central place in the scheme of things. As soon as he had lighted on such a theory the religious question was settled, for him, and it never troubled him again. He did not, however, hit on the central idea of *Life and Habit* until 1874, when he was thirty-eight ; and before that he had been through sixteen years of worrying things out, ever since, after taking his classical degree at Cambridge, he had begun to face the problem of his religious beliefs.

We have seen already how odd it was that he did not begin to do this sooner—the odder because he was in general so critical of his bringing up. It might have been expected that his attitude towards his father in other matters would have led him to some critical examination of his father's religion, which was the ostensible guide to all his doings, if not while he was at school, at least early in his undergraduate career. That it did not has been made clear ; and as we saw he went out of his way, in commenting on his Cambridge environment, to try to explain how this happened. The fact that his "doubts" came upon him late and suddenly, and faced him immediately with the great crisis of his life, partly accounts for the viciousness with which he turned on the upbringing that had brought him, utterly unwarned, into so dire a peril. He was convinced that it was his father's fault that he had not met sooner with the "infidel" case, and that it had been his father's duty both to put that case in his way and to answer it if he could. Canon Butler, no doubt, held it equally as his duty to do all he could to shield his children from "infidel" thoughts and contacts.

Even if Butler's view of what his father ought to have

5

done could be accepted, this would by no means make it possible to put all the blame on the Canon. Butler had been a boarder at a famous public school, and then four years at Cambridge ; and these institutions must surely bear a large part of the blame. Even if we acquit Shrewsbury, on the ground that it is a better thing for boys to get too little religion than too much, and that Dr. Kennedy may have been too busy with Latin Grammar to spare time for theology (though I am not saying that this was so), it remains extraordinary that Butler, as a young man intended for ordination, should have gone through four years at Cambridge without realising even that there were " infidels " of enough intellectual respectability to need to be taken into account. Yet we have to accept his statement that this is what happened ; and it seems clear from the shock he got when he did come up against " doubts " that it must have been as he said it was.

His " doubts " seem to have begun in a fashion ridiculous enough to have figured in his novel—though he did not in fact use the episode in *The Way of All Flesh*, having used it already for John Pickard Owen in *The Fair Haven*. Butler went, as we saw, to work for a time in a London slum parish as part of his preparation for ordination ; and there he made the discovery that a number of the boys in a class he was conducting had never been baptised. To his consternation, he was unable to discover any moral difference between those who had been baptised and those who had not ; and this disturbance to his faith in infant baptism soon spread to other things. In particular, he found Dean Alford's *Commentaries on the Gospels* most unsatisfactory ; for, after making it plain that the stories of the Resurrection and Ascension told by the four evangelists could not possibly be reconciled, the Dean in effect " recommended that the whole story should be taken on trust "—and this, Butler says in *The Way of All Flesh,* " Ernest was not prepared to do."

There is a singular *naïveté* about all this ; and even after Butler's account of conditions in Cambridge while he was an undergraduate we are left wondering how he managed to know so little. That he should not have been interested, until the need to prepare for ordination forced questions of doctrine on his attention, can be understood—though even that seems strange in so naturally questioning a person. That he should never have met an " infidel," or even have realised that there were such persons, except perhaps outside the ranks of gentlemen, is very much more curious. For, though the conflict between science and religion took a new lease of life with the publication of Darwin's *Origin of Species* in 1859, it was old history long before that ; and " infidelity " had, of course, a very much longer record still. The eighteenth century, in England as well as in France, had been full of it. The French Revolution had spread it over a very much wider field ; and in the first half of the nineteenth century it had been continuous, changing its emphasis from time to time, but never letting up for long.

According to Butler, at the time when he was at Cambridge, the very echoes of these lively controversies had died away, and nothing more serious than " dissent," which for the most part did not challenge the Scriptures and was in many respects more " fundamentalist " than the Church, worried the tranquillity of the Establishment. Even of Dissent he knew little ; for it was outside the pale of Cambridge and hardly troubled his father in his rural parish.

It was therefore possible for him to get to the very brink of ordination without ever seriously asking himself what he believed.

The Victorian age, at any rate till near its end, was a religious age, both in the sense that most people above the poverty line were religious, or took religion for granted, and also in the sense that a large proportion of them thought about many things in religious terms. In all probability, the unquestioning acceptance of religious dogma was at a higher point in the 1850s than it had been for well over a century, or than it has ever been since. England, by the middle of the century, appeared to have come singularly unscathed through the great period of " infidelity " associated with the French Revolution and the early nineteenth-century attacks on the Church. This was partly because something had been done towards reforming the Church, as well as the State, after 1832, so that the typical parson was much more earnest and hardworking than his predecessors had been, and the old attacks on ecclesiastical sinecurists, placemen and pluralists no longer cut the same amount of political ice as they had done in the days of Cobbett and Richard Carlile. By 1850 Carlile was quite forgotten, and Tom Paine's *Age of Reason* was no longer read save by a very few. Even the so-called " Rational Religion " of the followers of Robert Owen was near its death ; and though various brands of Secularism and Free Thought persisted in holes and corners they had no longer the power to trouble the calm of respectable society. On the whole, in working-class and near-working-class circles the religious counter-offensives had been remarkably successful.

The reason is to be sought mainly in the same causes as brought about the deep political tranquillity of the 'fifties

Chartism had ceased to command any more support after the fiasco of 1848 ; and the skilled workmen who had been the backbone both of Radicalism and of " infidelity "—two closely linked causes—were giving their minds to building up Trade Unions and Co-operative Societies on as peaceable a basis as was allowed them, and were turning away from the revolutionary politics that had brought only disillusionment and defeat. A part of the void thus created in the popular mind was being filled up by a great outburst of church-building and chapel-building. In every industrial town chapels were being built to house a wide variety of sects, new and old. Methodists predominated, but there was no limit to the number of different Bethels and Ebenezers that could find a devout following. Successful manufacturers salved their consciences for working their operatives long hours at low wages and for preaching and practising the workaday doctrine of " devil take the hindmost " by subscribing liberally towards the cause of religion ; and churchmen vied with dissenters in erecting new places of worship in the growing suburbs of the towns.

Geology, for a time, had seemed to offer a new and serious threat to the Mosaic account of the Creation and therewith to the foundations of religious orthodoxy. Lyell's *Geology*, which appeared in the early 1830s, had been followed ten years later by Robert Chambers's *Vestiges of the Natural History of Creation*, with its rationalistic treatment of the Old Testament story ; and in Germany the " higher criticism " of the New Testament had been developing fast since the publication of David Strauss's *Life of Jesus* in 1835. But these two intellectual attacks on the orthodox position had made no popular impact at all comparable with that of Paine's *Age of Reason* or even with that of Owenism.

There had been powerful counter-offensives from the religious side ; and on the whole the new schools of thought had made no impression on the working classes and very little higher up the social scale. Within the Church of England, the Evangelical movement, largely a response to the Methodist challenge, had spent most of its force before Butler's adolescence : the High Church party had been steadily gaining ground, but had been met with a new challenge from the Broad Churchmen inspired by Thomas Arnold and Frederick Maurice. Christian Socialism had its brief *floruit* in Butler's years of adolescence, but passed him by. His own grandfather, Bishop Samuel Butler, whose life he wrote in his latter years, had been a forerunner of the " Broad Church " view : his father, Thomas Butler, after some Evangelical leanings in his young days, had relapsed into a simple village clergyman whom the controversies of the day left untouched and unmoved.

The ferment of ideas set afoot by the French Revolution had affected the entire nation, because under the impact of the Industrial Revolution and of the long war the entire nation was being deeply stirred. The mood of unrest lasted for fully half a century ; for over all this time the common man was reacting continuously to being badgered about. Sometimes he reacted by taking up with some new brand of religion, the more fiery and millennarian the better : sometimes his reaction was violently anti-religious, comprehending Church and State, God and Government, in one and the same furious reaction against his lot and that of his fellow-sufferers. For the poor, all that half-century was an unhappy time. But after the crowning troubles of the early 'forties hope began to dawn for an increasing fraction even of the poorer people. The new capitalism was almost out of its growing pains ; and it was becoming in truth easier for men by industry and frugality to better their lot. A more acquiescent, because a more hopeful, mood began to take possession of the people. Chartism lost its appeal, and with the political *détente* went a corresponding relaxation of the popular controversies about religion, which came to be much less a political issue and much more, for the ordinary man, a matter of personal salvation, or even of social respectability.

With the mind of the poor, beyond the village of which his father was parson, Butler would in any event have had no direct contact as child, or schoolboy, or undergraduate. If, however, he had been born a few years sooner, he could hardly have escaped as thoroughly as he seems to have done the very knowledge that there was such a thing as " infidelity " to be reckoned with. For in the earlier part of the century, the disturbed state of the poor had affected the minds of the well-to-do, and even country parsons had not been immune from fears of rick-burning or similar signs of popular discontent, and had been usually ready enough to lay the blame on Tom Paine or Cobbett or other notorious enemies of the Established Church. By Butler's day, however, rick-burning and the fruitless struggle against the New Poor Law of 1834 were alike over and done with ; and in most areas the country parsons, though not those of the towns, could breathe freely in the assurance that in their terrain neither Methodists nor other kinds of Dissenters were gaining ground. Even the scare about " Papal Aggression " had receded from the clerical mind as the storm which accompanied Newman's secession to Rome died away. There was a religious as well as a political calm over England, or at least over that part of it which could be seen or heard

from Canon Butler's vicarage, or from Shrewsbury, or from
Cambridge University.

This was the calm before the storm ; for Darwin's *Origin
of Species* was soon to start the whole battle up again in a
new form, more challenging to orthodoxy than the attack
of the geologists because it centred round the historical
development of man himself. Butler, however, was not
led to " doubt " by Darwin, or by anything connected with
the march of science. His starting point was the " higher
criticism " of the Bible ; and what worried him above all
else was the plain inconsistency of the gospel narratives, or
rather the evident evasiveness of the scripture commentators
whose answers he, as a candidate for ordination, would be
called upon to reproduce. He read Darwin only later, in
New Zealand, when his critical faculties had already been
strongly aroused and when he had already put ordination
decisively behind him. Then, for a time, Darwin's influence
on him was great, and deeply upsetting ; for he did not at
all like the new scientific universe that was being offered
him as a substitute for the universe of religious faith.
Fundamentally, Butler was never a Darwinian critic of
religious dogma. His attack was based on the failure of the
scripture stories to agree, and on the doubt whether, in face
of their disagreement, there could be said to be any real
evidence at all for the essential dogmas of Christianity. Did
Christ rise from the dead ? All Christians, as far as Butler
knew, said that he did ; but had they any *rational* ground
for their belief ? It appeared to him that they had none.
Yet Strauss's theory that the apostles had believed in the
Resurrection and the Ascension, but had been the victims
of hallucination, failed to satisfy him. Certainly some of
them believed that they had seen Christ alive after the

Crucifixion. What if they had actually done so, but had seen, not a resurrected God, but a man who had not died? Was there any real evidence that Christ had *died* upon the Cross? That he had been crucified was probable enough; but had he died on the Cross or been taken down still alive? The more Butler studied the gospel stories, the more it looked to him as if this latter were the correct explanation. The time Christ hung on the Cross was not enough to account for death: there was nothing to show that the wound in his side had been mortal, or even dangerous. What if Joseph of Arimathea had taken him down living and had tended him secretly back to health? This seemed the more likely because, thereafter, we are told not a word more about Joseph, who simply disappears from all the stories. If Joseph had believed in Christ's Resurrection, surely he would have been heard of again. If he had every reason for not believing in it, he might very likely have kept quiet, and the silence of others about him would be explained. As for the Ascension, Butler found that there was no real evidence that the legend of it had arisen until much later; for hardly anyone still held that the Gospels had been written by the disciples whose names they bear, or until considerably later times. So, what if the whole story of Jesus could be accounted for without any miraculous element at all, simply as the growth of a legend among a credulous Eastern people?

This was the thesis Butler sustained in his anonymous pamphlet on *The Evidence for the Resurrection*, published in 1865, soon after his return from New Zealand, where he had worried the whole thing out for himself. And this pamphlet became the basis for his fuller exposition in *The Fair Haven*, and, much later, for his account of the growth

of " Sunchildism " in *Erewhon Revisited*. At first, when he
had weighed up the evidence as well as he could, he does
not appear fully to have realised how far he was being
carried. Indeed, he could not have made the sophistries of
The Fair Haven nearly so convincing had they not to a great
extent reproduced a mental journey which he had made for
himself in the solitude of his sheep-run on the Rangitata.
John Pickard Owen was never for a moment Butler ; but
many of his arguments were arguments which Butler had
tried out in his own mind, and had found wanting, and
some were even arguments with which he retained a good
deal of sympathy. For Butler, like his character, Owen,
believed after a fashion in a sort of a something that makes
for righteousness ; and, though he discarded more than he
made Owen discard, there was a residue common to the
author and to his character.

The Fair Haven is not a novel : it is a tract on theology.
But Butler made it partly a work of fiction by writing it,
not in his own person, but in that of an imaginary character,
John Pickard Owen, and by prefixing to it what purported
to be a memoir of the author by his brother, William
Bickersteth Owen, a devout admirer of John Pickard and of
his work. The supposed author had been at one time an
" unbeliever," and had come under the influence of Strauss's
Life of Jesus and of other writings of the " higher critics."
From this phase of infidelity he had come back to Christianity ; and in his book he was supposed to be retracing
for the benefit of his fellow-men the steps by which he had
been led first to " unbelief " and thereafter back to reasoned
belief. *The Fair Haven* purported, in its sub-title, to be " a
defence of the miraculous element in Our Lord's ministry
here on earth," but what the alleged defence came to in

substance was that the vital part of Christianity would stand unaffected even if all belief in the supposedly miraculous elements in it were to be given up. John Pickard Owen was made to argue throughout that those who, like Dean Alford in his edition of the Gospels, attempted to gloss over discrepancies in the Bible story or to disguise the weaknesses in Christian " evidences " were no true friends of religion, which could lay claim to no acceptance except on a basis reconcilable with human reason.

The tract part of *The Fair Haven* is still eminently worth reading by anyone who is interested in Christian " evidences." For the reader who is prepared to accept the criteria of ordinary common sense as applicable to the problems of religious belief it sets out what remains a very cogent case. But for students of Butler as a novelist the thing is the pre- fatory *Memoir* of the imaginary John Pickard Owen. This is excellent fooling, and contains delightfully told stories designed to illustrate John Pickard's instinctive love of truth. There is, first, the tale of the lady visitor who was put to sleep in the nursery and, on the first night, finding John Pickard and his brother awake, prayed sonorously for them, but on a subsequent evening, when they pretended to be asleep, did not say her prayers at all, and after that prayed only on evenings when she believed them awake. Butler got this story from Miss Savage, to whom it had actually occurred ; but it was his own touch to add the point that this experience first taught the children, to their infinite relief, that there was hope of not having to say bed-time prayers all the days of their life. Butler, as William Bicker- steth Owen, appends " It is needless to add that we had the matter out with her before she left, and that the consequences were unpleasant for all parties ; they added to the troubles in which we were already involved as to our prayers, and were indirectly among the earliest causes which led my brother to look with scepticism upon religion."

There is a second story, of the same lady visitor, in even broader vein. Here it is, in words put into the mouth of William Bickersteth Owen :

> " I remember that this was the occasion on which my brother discovered a good many things in connection with the fair sex which had hitherto been beyond his ken ; more especially that the mass of petticoats and clothes which envelop the female form were not, as he expressed it to me, ' all solid woman,' but that women were not in reality more substantially built than men, and had legs as much as he had, a fact which he had never yet realised. On this he for a long time considered them as impostors, who had wronged him by leading him to suppose that they had far more ' lady in them ' (so he said) than he now found they had. This was a sort of thing which he regarded with stern moral reprobation."

I quote this, not only for its own sake, but also to show how much Butler's contemporaries were ready to swallow under the aegis of moralising ; for despite this anecdote and others like it, *The Fair Haven* was taken quite seriously, John Pickard Owen and all, by quite a number of eminent Christian leaders. It was, indeed, no more outrageous than a great deal of contemporary tract-writing in biographical form.

The gem of the *Memoir* prefixed to *The Fair Haven* is the account of Mrs. Owen, mother of the Owen brothers—an advance sketch, on more farcical lines, of the Christina of *The Way of All Flesh*, and undoubtedly a caricature of one aspect of Butler's own mother.

> " She had become deeply impressed with the millennarian fervour which laid hold of so many some twenty-five years

ago. The Apocalypse was perhaps her favourite book in the Bible, and she was imbued with the fullest conviction that all the threatened horrors with which it teems were upon the eve of their accomplishment. The year eighteen hundred and forty-eight was to be (as indeed it was) a time of general bloodshed and confusion, while in eighteen hundred and sixty-six, should it please God to spare her, her eyes would be gladdened by the visible descent of the Son of Man with a shout, with the voice of the Archangel, with the trump of God ; and the dead in Christ should rise first ; then she, as one of them that were alive, would be caught up with other saints into the air, and would possibly receive while rising some distinguishing token of confidence and approbation which should fall with due impressiveness upon the surrounding multitude ; then would come the consummation of all things, and she would be ever with the Lord. She died peaceably in her bed before she could know that a commercial panic was the nearest approach to the fulfilment of prophecy which the year eighteen hundred and sixty-six brought forth."

This exalted mother, we are told, became convinced that her two children were to be the two witnesses mentioned in the Book of Revelation.

" We therefore," says W. B. Owen, " made a careful examination of the passage which threw light upon our future ; but on finding that the prospect was gloomy and full of bloodshed we protested against the honours which were intended for us, especially when we reflected that the mother of the two witnesses was not menaced in Scripture with any particular discomfort. . . . Her notion clearly was that we were to be massacred somewhere in the streets of London, in consequence of the anti-Christian machinations of the Pope ; that after lying about unburied for three days and a half we were to come to life again ; and, finally, that we should auspiciously ascend to heaven, in front, perhaps, of the Foundling Hospital."

Readers of *The Way of All Flesh* will remember that Christina was greatly given to this kind of day-dreaming.

with reference both to her husband and to her children ;
and there is no doubt at all that Butler took the trait from
his own mother, just as he is known to have taken the letter
to her children which Christina wrote when she believed
herself dying—and kept by her till she did die. That Butler
could thus poke fun at his mother while she was still alive
—she died in the year in which *The Fair Haven* was published—is strange, and Butler himself felt the need to excuse
it. He made W. B. Owen write, " I have given the above
in its more amusing aspect, and am half afraid that I may
appear to be making a jest of weakness on the part of one
of the most devotedly unselfish mothers who have ever
existed. But one can love while smiling." It is indisputable
that he was taken aback by the deep offence which this part
of his book gave to his sisters, and wrote in his private letters
words which almost imply that he had expected them to see
and enjoy the joke. This was curious insensitiveness in a
man whose whole record shows that he was both abnormally
sensitive, or even " touchy," in relation to his own affairs
and unusually fearful of saying or doing anything that might
give offence to those whom he reckoned among his friends.
In relation to his family's feelings Butler had a blind spot.
He might not have minded paining his father or sisters,
when he thought they deserved it ; but it gave him remorse
when he felt that he had really pained his mother by taking
her off. This did not deter him from taking her off again
as Christina ; but by then she was dead and in his view not
in a position to mind.

All in all, the *Memoir* of John Pickard Owen is one of
the most amusing things Butler ever wrote. It inspired
Miss Savage, who enjoyed it immensely, to keep on at him
that he must write a real novel ; and under this stimulus

The Way of All Flesh was begun. It was almost certainly at her instigation that he read George Eliot's *Middlemarch*, published in the same year as *Erewhon*, in order to get the measure of the well-considered contemporary novel of ideas. He did not like it. He wrote to Miss Savage, " I call it bad and not interesting : there is no sweetness in the whole book." . . . " The book seems to me to be a long-winded piece of studied brag, clever enough, I daresay, but to me at any rate singularly unattractive."

Butler could not possibly have liked the solemnity of *Middlemarch*. Perhaps his study of it did something, by contraries, to set the tone for *The Way of All Flesh*. George Eliot, as well as Butler, had been influenced by Strauss's *Life of Jesus* : they were both " higher critics." But, with Butler, the " higher criticism " took a humorous turn which the author of *Middlemarch* would have appreciated as little as he did her masterpiece. Butler often complained that his contemporaries did not appreciate his work. He liked theirs quite as little.

CHAPTER V

EREWHON

EREWHON, or, Over the Range, published in 1872, is the story of an imaginary journey to an unknown country, cut off completely from contact with the rest of the world. *Erewhon,* of course, is " Nowhere " written backwards ; and its customs were mainly inversions of those of the Victorian England which Butler was setting out to satirise. In Erewhon what we call crime was regarded as a form of disease needing medical attention and calling for sympathy, whereas what we call disease was treated, and punished, as serious crime. In Erewhon, machinery, instead of being worshipped as the source from which all blessings flow, was execrated and forbidden. In Erewhon there were two kinds of banks and currency—one used for real business transactions and the other—the " Musical Banks " and their token money—merely for show and pretence. Erewhon was Victorian England back to front ; and the result was very amusing.

Erewhon was Butler's one commercially successful book ; and even its success was very modest. Its author was also usually very modest about its merits, and inclined sometimes to depreciate it severely. That, however, was when he was contrasting its reception with that of other works, such as *Life and Habit,* which he held to be of much greater importance, or when, in his letters, he was combating Miss Savage's evident desire to turn him into a regular purveyor of three-decker novels. Really, Butler, at any rate in later life, thought quite well of his " first book "—for he always refused to count *A First Year in Canterbury Settlement* and preferred to call *Erewhon* his " Op. 1." He said of *Erewhon* in his preface to the revised edition of 1901 that there was " no central idea underlying it " ; and that there was " hardly any story, and little attempt to give life and individuality to the characters." He added his hope that in *Erewhon Revisited* " both these defects have been in great measure avoided." " *Erewhon*," he wrote, " was not an organic whole ; *Erewhon Revisited* may fairly claim to be one. Nevertheless, though in literary workmanship I do not doubt that this last-named book is an improvement on the first, I shall be agreeably surprised if I am not told that *Erewhon*, with all its faults, is the better reading of the two."

In general, these judgments and anticipations are quite correct. *Erewhon* is not a story, with some philosophical quirks and observations thrown in : it is a series of humorously expressed moral and social judgments with a story built round them. In *Erewhon*, the characters have almost no individuality : they are at most types, not persons. In this respect, the contrast with *Erewhon Revisited* is quite startling : the later book also has its types, but even Hanky and Panky are given quite a bit of individuality, and the entire household of Yram is alive and personal from the first moment to the last. Nearly all the people in *Erewhon Revisited* appear to come alive as soon as one meets them, whereas in *Erewhon* it was plainly never in the author's intention to attempt to make any of them come alive at all. The characters of the earlier *Erewhon* were pegs to hang thoughts on : those of *Erewhon Revisited* were thought of and felt as real people.

6

Nevertheless, Butler was not wrong in supposing that the public would for the most part prefer *Erewhon* to its sequel. *Erewhon* might have been a better book if the characters had had more life in them ; but it might have been a worse book if the living characters had got in the way of Butler's exposition of Erewhonian philosophy, which was after all its main point. It is not easy to combine effective satire, which is much concerned with types, with effective characterisation. Butler managed this in *The Way of All Flesh* because there he was using real individuals whom he made to stand for types. In *Erewhon* he was not using real people, or even people of his imagination. How far he consciously used real people for the characters of *Erewhon Revisited* I do not pretend to know, though I fancy that his Swiss friend, Hans Faesch,[1] may have sat in part for George's portrait and that some of his Italian and Sicilian friends got into the picture somehow. The real difference, however, was that the " philosophical " part of *Erewhon Revisited*—that is, all the account of the " Sunchild " myth and of its development —while it took up a great part of the book, could be in the main isolated from his pictures of the people. For of course Butler did not make George, any more than Yram and her husband, believe in the miraculous elements of the Sunchild story ; and therefore he could keep them out of it as he could not the Nosnibors or the other shadowy people who occupy the stage in *Erewhon*.

The impersonality of *Erewhon* was indeed implicit in the manner of its writing, which was spread over " something like ten years." The book was written, Butler says, " with great difficulty." Nor is it only a question of the time taken. The writing of *Erewhon* began with the article, *Darwin*

---

[1] See page 101.

among the Machines, that Butler published in New Zealand in
1863, and rewrote and enlarged for Holyoake's *Reasoner*
in 1865. The next part to be written was *The World of the
Unborn*, in or about 1865, and then came, almost immediately,
the first sketch of *The Musical Banks* and of the trial of a
man for being in consumption. All these were written as
separate articles, with no idea of making them into a book.
The suggestion of doing so came from F. N. Broome, a
friend of Butler's, in 1870 ; and *Erewhon* was written on
Sundays in the later months of 1870 and the early months
of 1871, while Butler was working hard at painting all the
rest of the week.

Thus, the story of *Erewhon* was literally written round the
articles. All the opening part, the journey across the great
range of hills and the description of the country, including
the very amusing description of Chowbok, came nearly
straight out of Butler's own experiences in New Zealand,
suitably—and very effectively—touched up. The rest was
imagination, but with a touch in the Erewhonian country
of the Italian visits of Butler's boyhood. It was imagination,
but imagination working to shape, with the object of con-
structing a framework within which the satires on materialist
science, on " musical bank " religion, and on parents and
children could lie together comfortably without jostling. It
is a notable fact that these three things were the main substance of what Butler already wanted to say at this stage.
From *The Book of the Machines* in *Erewhon* stem off all his
later books on creative evolution ; from *The Musical Banks*
come his attacks on false religion ; and from *The World of
the Unborn* is derived the handling of the problem of parent-
hood in *The Way of All Flesh*. Butler's ideas were still
unmatured when he wrote *Erewhon* ; but in essence they

were all there, or at least were all being searched for. He had not yet hit on the theory of *Life and Habit*; but he was in chase of it, and was not happy till he found it.

The Book of the Machines is in substance an onslaught on the false use of analogy. He had a deep distrust of analogical argument—though, like all of us, he sometimes fell into it. He was fully convinced that the notion of human beings, or indeed of any living things, being " just like " machines was all wrong ; and he took his usual course with every false-hood he met with. He turned it inside out, or upside down, and saw what it looked like reversed. Many of the scientists were saying that men were " just like " machines. Very well : how about seeing what would follow if one affirmed instead that machines were " just like " men ? Butler tried it, and found that it worked perfectly—to a conclusion just as absurdly logical as if one began the other way round. Moreover, the working out of this idea gave him part of the setting for his story : he had to have a country with a culture not based on machinery, and yet capable of philo-sophising about it with knowledge. Clearly, then, he needed a country which had once developed a civilisation founded on machinery, but, like William Morris's later " Nowhere," had got rid of it.

This took him a stage further ; for such a country could have most of the characteristics of Victorian England, except the industrialism, which in any case he would not have known how to handle. So the Musical Banks could fit in comfortably as a satire on church-going morality ; and with the Musical Banks could come in a great deal of the Victorian respectability against which Butler was in revolt. Ydgrun and Ydgrunism arrived close in the wake of the Musical Banks, and with them came the setting for the family life

of the Nosnibors. Butler did not, however, make Mr.
Nosnibor into a clergyman : nor, singularly enough, did the
King Charles's head of Canon Butler even poke its nose into
the story. Mr. Nosnibor had to be a business man, in order
to get the requisite sharp contrast between the " Musical
Bank " religion of the ladies and the real working faith of
Erewhonian manhood.

There remained to be worked in the trial of the man
taken in consumption ; and this too fitted quite neatly. It
could be linked on to Mr. Nosnibor's business affairs, at the
cheap price of making him a swindler, and allowing him to
be commiserated with on his lapse from virtue (which was
not represented as habitual), so as to get the needed contrast
between Erewhonian and Victorian notions of physical and
moral health. If Butler had been writing *Erewhon* a few
years later, he would probably not have been able to treat
Mr. Nosnibor's business affairs with quite so light a touch.
After his own experiences and the loss of his money in and
after 1874 he developed a thorough-going horror of slipshod
business habits and of speculation. One of the choruses in
his *Narcissus* oratorio runs

> " O Speculation ! horrid fiend,
>   Full well we know thee now,
> The mask that erst thy features screened
>   Has fallen from thy brow."

But when he was writing *Erewhon* Henry Hoare's companies
still seemed to be going well. Almost any fool could make
money, or feel as if he were making it, in 1872 and 1873—
the great boom years before the great Victorian slump, that
taught our grandfathers to think twice and to be a great
deal more careful with their money than they had been

during the great expansion. Moral health on the part of business men was a sorer subject with Butler after his own financial crash and his years of vain struggle in Canada to get at any rate some of his money back.

The touch in *Erewhon* was light ; but on the questions of physical and moral health much of Butler's Erewhonian philosophy was quite remarkably prescient ; it gives him a clear place among the forerunners of modern psychology ; and it is a little surprising that it never occurred to him later on to continue chasing this particular clue. If Freud had written a little earlier, one wonders what Butler would have made of him. He might have been started off on another Odyssey as extensive as that which he was provoked to by *The Origin of Species*.

There are in *Erewhon*, besides the philosophical strands already mentioned as drawn out of earlier articles, two other strands which may, or may not, have had a similar origin. These are the Colleges of Unreason and the views of the Erewhonian philosophers on the rights of animals and of vegetables. The Colleges of Unreason, and the system of " hypothetics " taught therein, together with the account of the importance given to the " hypothetical language," are obviously drawn from Butler's experience of Shrewsbury— the most strictly " classical " of all public schools in Butler's day under Kennedy, as it had been under his own grandfather —and of Cambridge.

> " The store they set by this hypothetical language can hardly be believed ; they will even give anyone a maintenance for life if he attains a considerable proficiency in the study of it ; nay, they will spend years in learning to translate some of their own good poetry into the hypothetical language—to do so with fluency being reckoned a distinguishing mark of a scholar and a gentleman. Heaven forbid that I should be flippant, but

it appeared to me to be a wanton waste of good human energy that men should spend years and years in the perfection of so barren an exercise, when their own civilisation presented problems by the hundred which cried aloud for solution and would have paid the solver handsomely ; but people know their own affairs best. If the youths chose it for themselves I should have wondered less ; but they do not choose it ; they have it thrust upon them, and for the most part are disinclined towards it. I can only say that all I heard in defence of the system was insufficient to make me think very highly of its advantages."

This is straight criticism of " a classical education " ; but Butler's account of the study of " Unreason " is a mingling of paradox with his own opinions. He puts quite a strong case—and one that is highly characteristic of him—into the mouths of the Professors of Unreason.

"Life, they urge, would be intolerable if men were to be guided in all they did by reason and reason only. Reason betrays men into the drawing of hard and fast lines, and to the defining by language—language being like the sun, which rears and then scorches. Extremes are alone logical, but they are always absurd ; the mean is illogical, but an illogical mean is better than the sheer absurdity of an extreme."

This is Butler's philosophy of commonsense, which he recurs to again and again in *The Way of All Flesh*. He juggles with the idea of reason as he did with the idea of God.

"The Professors of Unreason deny that they undervalue reason : none can be more convinced than they are, that if the double currency cannot be rigorously deduced as a necessary consequence of human reason, the double currency should cease forthwith ; but they say that it must be deduced from no narrow and exclusive view of reason which should deprive that admirable faculty of one-half of its own existence. Unreason is a part of reason : it must therefore be allowed its full share in stating the initial conditions."

That was why there was a Professor of Worldly Wisdom at
the College of Unreason which Mr. Higgs visited ; and the
Professor, in arguing with his visitor, was allowed to score
some good hits.

> " I ventured feebly to say that I did not see how progress
> could be made in any art or science, or indeed in anything at
> all, without more or less self-seeking, and hence unamiability.
> ' Of course it cannot,' said the Professor, ' and therefore we
> object to progress.' "

There is much more that is amusing in Butler's description
of the typical " don "—not least in his account of the college
professors' fear of giving themselves away by saying what
they thought, so that Higgs " found it difficult to get definite
opinions from any of them, except on such subjects as the
weather, eating and drinking, holiday excursions, or games
of skill."

As for the rights of animals, and of vegetables, all that
part bears signs of later writing than the rest, and serves
mainly to drive home the lesson that it is unwise to press on
to logical conclusions, except with the purpose of recoiling
from them, as he represented the Erewhonians as having
done when, after giving up meat-eating, they came to realise
that no sharp line could be drawn between the lives of
animals and plants. Chesterton, with his " Why should
salt suffer ? " in *The Napoleon of Notting Hill*, pressed
the conclusion farther, into the realm of the inorganic,
with the same moral—that the illogical is preferable to
the absurd.

Finally, there is Ydgrun, the goddess of whom " even her
most devoted worshippers were a little ashamed," because
she was sometimes both cruel and absurd. Butler defended
Ydgrun, with reservations.

" Take her all in all, however, she was a beneficent and useful diety, who did not care how much she was denied so long as she was obeyed and feared, and who kept hundreds of thousands in those paths which make life tolerably happy, who would never have been kept there otherwise, and over whom a higher and more spiritual ideal would have had no power."

Butler, in his personal doings, was a good deal of an Ydgrunite. He flouted Mrs. Grundy openly only pen in hand, and never in overt deeds. He entirely meant what he said when he wrote that

" the gradual raising of the popular conception of Ydgrun would be the greatest spiritual boon which could be conferred upon them "—the Erewhonians—and that " nothing could effect this except example." Those whom he called the " high Ydgrunites " he described as " gentlemen in the full sense of the word ; and what has one not said in saying this ? " He added that such persons " seldom spoke of Ydgrun, or even alluded to her, but would never run counter to her dictates without ample reason for doing so." In such cases, however, " they would override her with due self-reliance, and the goddess seldom punished them ; for they are brave, and Ydgrun is not."

This was pretty near to Butler's ideal of behaviour, to which he lived up except as a writer. But there was a sprite in his pen, and he never ceased to be surprised when people took amiss what it had led him on to say. Not that he repudiated what he had said, or repented of it : he somehow thought that the written word did not count in at all the same way as the deed, or as the same word spoken in mixed company ; and, timid usually in his social behaviour, he had claws like a tiger's when he got back home and wrote it all down.

Erewhon Revisited, except for Professors Hanky and Panky, Professor Gargoyle, and a few other not very important

characters, is a quite different sort of book, and much less a
satire. In it Butler makes his visitor to Erewhon, Mr. Higgs,
go back in order to see, thirty years later, what has happened
to the country since he made his escape from it in a balloon
which the Queen had allowed him to have built. Mr. Higgs
found, much to his consternation—for Butler chose to
represent him as a simple-minded, zealous Christian—that
during his absence he had been made into a God, and his
balloon ascent transformed into a miraculous reception into
Heaven by means of a chariot drawn by fiery black horses—
some of whose ordure was preserved as a holy relic. He
had been named " The Sunchild " ; and " Sunchildism "
had become the official Erewhonian religion, having been
taken up and skilfully developed by the directors of the
" Musical Banks," who had thus given their declining cult
a new and vigorous lease of life. The story of the growth
of this new religion, and of the accretion of miracles round
the central miracle, provides the main theme of *Erewhon
Revisited* ; and the theme is skilfully introduced by setting
the two Professors, Hanky and Panky, to talk about it in
Mr. Higgs's presence before his identity is suspected. How
Mr. Higgs attended the official opening of a temple erected
to his own glory, and attempted, with no success, to undo
the mischief he had unwittingly done, the reader must be
left to discover for himself. My point is that the presence
of this central theme affects the entire treatment, and reduces
the satire both to a secondary place and to a much less
pungent criticism of contemporary society. Even when
Butler returns, in *Erewhon Revisited,* to the old themes, he
usually handles them quite differently. Mrs. Humdrum acts
in the spirit of the Colleges of Unreason ; but she does so
in a thoroughly human way, and comes to life in doing so.

Even Dr. Downie, though more shadowy, is a human being ; and the religion of Ydgrunism seems to have undergone the earlier stages of the process of transformation to its " higher " form that Butler desired. There is less satire in *Erewhon Revisited* because in a sense its central theme *is* satire, and this leaves less scope for other satire by the way. But it is less satirical also because Yram, the Mayor, her husband, George, who is Higgs's son by Yram, and even Mrs. Humdrum are portrayed without a touch of satire, as thoroughly nice and pleasant people, who have succeeded admirably by putting the Butlerian philosophy of the mean into practical effect.

So the satire is all, or nearly all, concentrated on the Sunchild myth, which as we have seen is a new version of a part of what Butler had written in *The Fair Haven* nearly thirty years before. In *The Fair Haven* he had been concerned not only to deny that there was any good evidence of Christ having *died* on the Cross, but also to argue that the story of Christ's Ascension could very easily have grown out of very small beginnings. In *Erewhon Revisited* he did not follow quite the same, or so plausible a line ; for Higgs's ascent in a balloon was certainly not a small beginning at all like the two Marys mistaking the white grave-cloths in the darkened grave for angels. Butler, in his later book, concentrated rather on the elaboration of the legend, and on the part played by the Musical Banks, after they had seen its possibilities, in securing its acceptance and in decorating it for popular consumption.

Butler was shocked when he was told that some people supposed him to have intended to draw any personal parallel between Jesus Christ and Mr. Higgs, the Sunchild ; and obviously no such comparison had been meant. It was with the story of the Ascension and not with Christ's personality that Butler was concerned, and he had no idea that readers would be shocked in that particular way, though he of course expected them still to be shocked by his entire theory, as their fathers and mothers had been by *The Fair Haven* a generation earlier.

I suppose that *Erewhon Revisited* is not much liked nowadays because the main argument is now so familiar as not to keep the attention, and the rest, good as it is, is not weighty enough to bear the whole burden. Personally, I like it a great deal, because the pictures of Yram and the Mayor and George attract me ; but I can see why others find it, as well as most of *The Fair Haven,* dull. Both books date, in most readers' reactions to them, in a quite different fashion from that in which *The Way of All Flesh* dates. Their central themes date, whereas the central themes of *The Way of All Flesh,* subject to secondary modifications, are of all time.

CHAPTER VI

LOVES AND LIKINGS

GOOD as the *Erewhon* books are, Butler, as a novelist, stands or falls by *The Way of All Flesh*. The book, published only after his death, is in a sense his spiritual autobiography. He put into it, altering the form but keeping the substance as he interpreted it, the story of his own youth and subsequent emancipation. No doubt he made Ernest Pontifex, whose history the book relates, experience some extremes which he had not suffered in his own person. Ernest was made to go through with ordination, whereas Butler had the strength of mind to draw back. Ernest was sent to prison for an indecent assault on a virtuous woman—whereas it seems to be well established that Butler, at Ernest's age, knew a great deal too much to have been likely to fall into such a mistake. By way of compensation, Butler equipped Ernest with a fairy-godmother, who, when, like Butler, he had lost his money by speculation, left him (though he was not allowed to know it at once) very comfortably endowed. Butler's reversion to the Whitehall property was thus transformed for the purposes of the story, and Ernest was allowed to come into his money a good deal sooner than his creator got to the end of his own financial difficulties.

The Way of All Flesh is good from beginning to end ; but I think a good many people will agree that the best part of it is the part that is not autobiographical, but relates to a time before Ernest Pontifex was born. The sketch of

93

old George Pontifex, Ernest's grandfather, the religious bookseller and domestic tyrant in the grand manner, is delightful. Nothing could better his indignation at being served with lobster salad made with a cock instead of a hen lobster, or his breaking the bottle containing water from the Jordan which he had reserved for his grandson's christening, and then telling an unblushing falsehood about it in his butler's presence. No less masterly is the account of the lives of Theobald and Christina, Ernest's father and mother, including the scene in the carriage after the wedding, when he first asserted his marital authority by commanding her to order the dinner at the hotel for which they were bound. When she asked to be let off,

> " The loving smile departed from his face, and was succeeded by a scowl which that old Turk, his father, might have envied. ' Stuff and nonsense, my dearest Christina,' he exclaimed mildly, and stamped his foot upon the floor of the carriage. ' It is a wife's duty to order her husband's dinner ; you are my wife, and I shall expect you to order mine.' "

Then follows an account of the thoughts that passed through Theobald's mind—he had never meant to marry the woman : " he had not married her ; it was all a hideous dream ; he would—but a voice kept ringing in his ears which said : ' YOU CAN'T, CAN'T, CAN'T.' " And then, of course, Christina burst into tears, and promised to order the dinner after all ; and the situation was saved. Theobald breathed again.

> " After a few moments more he drew her towards him, kissed away her tears, and assured her that he knew she would be a good wife to him.
> ' Dearest Theobald,' she exclaimed in answer, ' you are an angel.' "

All this part of the book is the best kind of farce—farce with a serious meaning. It is quite admirably done—and all out of Butler's head for once ; for he can hardly have been privy to what his father and mother said to each other as they drove away from their wedding.

Then comes all the part about Ernest's boyhood. What relates to his affairs at home has been discussed in a previous chapter. His school life remains throughout rather shadowy, the light being mostly spotted on his relations with his aunt, Alethea, Theobald's sister, who took him up and was kind to him. One gets nowhere any clear impression of Butler's school-days. All one knows is that in later life he turned into a devoted " old boy," faithfully attending the annual Shrewsbury dinner, and even on at least one occasion getting the boys a half-holiday when he visited the school. There is, of course, the inimitable picture of the headmaster, Dr. Skinner, said to be based on Benjamin Hall Kennedy, who succeeded Bishop Butler at Shrewsbury. "Dr. Skinner," he writes, apropos of a later visit to the school, " was one of those who pride themselves on being able to set people at their ease at once, and I had been sitting on the edge of my chair all the evening." And then there is the episode of Dr. Skinner's supper.

" ' What will you take for supper, Dr. Skinner ? ' said Mrs. Skinner in a silvery voice.

He made no answer for some time, but at last, in a tone of almost superhuman solemnity, he said, first, ' Nothing,' and then ' Nothing whatever.'

By and by, however, I had a sense come over me as though I was nearer the consummation of all things than I had ever yet been. The room seemed to grow dark, as an expression came over Dr. Skinner's face, which showed that he was about to speak. The expression gathered force, the room grew

darker and darker. ' Stay,' he at length added, and I felt that
here at any rate was an end to a suspense which was rapidly
becoming unbearable. ' Stay—I may presently take a glass of
cold water—and a small piece of bread and butter.' "

After this, it is hardly necessary to add, the doctor made an
excellent meal off oysters, minced veal, apple tart, and a
hunk of bread and cheese.

To Butler's schooldays no doubt belongs the delightful
matron, Mrs. Jay, who

" rushed in with her spectacles on her forehead and her cap
strings flying, and called the boy whom Ernest had selected
as his hero the ' rampingest—scampingest—rackety—tackety—
tow—row—roaringest boy in the whole school.' "

The central figure of Ernest's schooldays, however, is his
aunt Alethea. Alethea is, and yet is not, Eliza Mary Ann
Savage, who might, and again might not, be called the only
begetter of The Way of All Flesh. Butler's acquaintance
with Miss Savage—he always addressed her and, I am sure,
thought of her as " Miss Savage," with no Eliza and no Mary
Ann—began characteristically, with the lady he supposed
" always trying to snub him" and " disliking him very much."
They were art-students together then, at Heatherley's ;
and probably Miss Savage was not trying to snub Butler at
all, but was only giving vent to some of the tart little
witticisms that plentifully pepper her letters. Butler, having
a skin too few, took her humorous threats as directed against
himself. He was at that stage afraid of young women of
his own class, even if they were dowdy, as Miss Savage
unquestionably was. This was not because he did not like
women. On the contrary, he was strongly sexed all his
life, and had need of them ; but he preferred a mistress,

whom he could keep apart from his everyday life, to anyone who might disturb the peace of his bachelor chambers. He maintained continuous relations with Madame Lucie Dumas from 1872 to her death in 1892 ; but fifteen years passed before he disclosed his real name to her.

Sexual need being thus satisfied, Butler was quite ready for a sexless friendship with Miss Savage, when once, somehow or other, the barrier between them had been broken down. Butler says it was " some years " before she got to like him, and the surviving correspondence between them begins only in 1871, the earlier letters having been destroyed. By 1871 they were evidently on close terms of friendship ; and they wrote to each other, and met often, right up to her death in 1885. But he was always " Mr. Butler" to her, as she was "Miss Savage" to him; and he certainly never wished or would have had it otherwise. As for her, who shall say ? Butler convinced himself later on that she had wanted to marry him ; and possibly he was right. But he certainly misunderstood the words of hers on which he laid stress as revealing this ; and the point remains in doubt. It is, to say the least, quite on the cards that Miss Savage, who was lame and a sufferer from hip disease as well as dowdy, knew perfectly well from the outset that marriage was not for her, and got all the kick she looked for out of being Butler's literary friend and confidant. Certainly she admired his talents hugely, and her letters gently show that she was not blind to his personal faults. After her death, Butler reproached himself for the egoism which his own letters revealed in his side of the relationship, and said that he had taken all he wanted from her and had given her nothing in return. The egoism was certainly there ; but it remains possible that Butler, though he knew it not, was

7

giving the "little, lame lady" all she wanted of him, or at all events all she ever allowed herself to hope for.

Butler's gain from the friendship was immense. Without it, he would certainly never have written *The Way of All Flesh*, which he could never bear to touch again after her death. In her letters, she gave better than she got; and from them came the germ of a good many of Butler's best notions and phrases. Passing her life between clubs and societies of emancipated women, for which she acted as secretary and manager, and a home which she found depressing, with continual exaction of chores and repressions by one ailing and one very exacting parent,[1] Miss Savage lived a vivid half-imaginary existence as Butler's correspondent, delighting to credit herself with vices which she did not possess, such as *gourmandise*, lying and laziness, and egging Butler on to say everything he could be induced to say about Victorian home life, Victorian religion, and Victorian complacency. Miss Savage, quite as much as Butler, enjoyed feeling naughty; and they corresponded in the spirit of naughty children doing and plotting dreadful things together behind Mr. and Mrs. Grundy's back. No man was ever so fortunate as Butler in his Egeria; and no doubt Egerias are at their most satisfactory when there is a Phryne somewhere handy who can be called upon when the spirit needs a change.

Alethea, in *The Way of All Flesh*, appears as Theobald Pontifex's sister and Ernest Pontifex's fairy-godmother aunt. Unlike Miss Savage, she is rich and beautiful—both high virtues in Butler's eyes—and stays single not for lack of offers but by choice. For the rest she is Miss Savage, toned down

---

[1] Miss Savage was very fond of her father, but disliked her mother, who seems to have been something of a feminine Theobald.

somewhat from the sprightliness of the correspondence, but in essentials the same. Not that Miss Savage, when she read and criticised Butler's novel, ever dropped a hint of knowing that she had sat for Alethea's portrait, though doubtless she was well aware of it. One of Miss Savage's highest qualities was a remarkably acute perception of what not to say.

In the novel Alethea appears as a " sport," or apparently causeless variation, in the Pontifex species. If Butler had revised his story again after suffering his change of heart about his grandfather the bishop, to whom he raised so pious a monument in his worst book,[1] he would no doubt have made Alethea very much the daughter of the transfigured old George Pontifex. But then Theobald and Christina would have been left unexplained by heredity ; and that would never have done. The story had to stay as it was, because, if the author had taken it to pieces again, he would never have been able to rebuild it. So Alethea had to remain as a " *lusus naturae* " ; and, even if that puts Butler into the very fix which he attributed to Darwin, few will argue that his novel is any the worse for that.

Alethea, in the story, sets out to watch over Ernest Pontifex, in the hope of making amends to him for his parents' shortcomings. She does him endless good while she lives, and in nothing more than in leaving him her money, under Overton's charge, when she dies. She is made to have a close platonic friendship with Overton, the narrator of the story, who is one of Butler's self-portraits ; and their friendship is obviously based on his own with Miss Savage. " It is impossible for me to explain," Overton is made to write, " how it was that she and I never married.

[1] *The Life and Letters of Dr. Samuel Butler.*

We two knew exceedingly well, and that must suffice for the reader. There was the most perfect sympathy and understanding between us ; we knew that neither of us would marry anyone else." So far, so good ; but then Overton is made to continue, " I had asked her to marry me a dozen times over ; having said this much I will say no more upon a point which is in no way necessary for the development of my story." Assuredly, Butler never asked Miss Savage to marry him. He made that quite clear in the sonnets which he wrote about her after she was dead.

> " A man will yield for pity, if he can,
>   But, if the flesh rebels, what can he do ? "

and again,

> " I liked, but like and love are far removed ;
>   Hard though I tried to love, I tried in vain.
>   For she was plain and lame and fat and short,
>   Forty and over-kind. Hence it befell
>   That though I loved her in a certain sort,
>   Yet did I love too wisely but not well."

Here I think Butler was deceiving himself and, out of his adopted character, sentimentalising at the same moment as he displayed his outrageous candour. I do not believe he ever tried to love Miss Savage in a marrying way, or indeed in any way that is called " love " where men and women of a near age are concerned. He liked Miss Savage immensely : she was the greatest of comforts to him : he needed her as much as he needed his trousers. But love her ? Not he.

Nor, probably, did he love " Madame," as he always called Lucie Dumas. He was fond of her, in a different way, and needed her too. But the only people he ever loved were Pauli and, much later, a young Swiss named Hans Faesch, with whom he fell quite romantically in love in 1893, the year after " Madame's " death. The only thoroughly sentimental thing Butler ever wrote was his Whitmanesque poem about Hans Faesch when the young man emigrated to the Far East in 1895—two years after their first meeting. That was an old man's affection for a young one : the Pauli affair began when both he and Butler were young. But Butler's love for Pauli was from the first a one-sided thing : it seems clear that Pauli never cared a button for him, except as a convenience. Yet he stuck to Pauli, despite every rebuff, for well over thirty years. Butler, in effect, never liked and loved and desired all in one. He kept the three things in three quite separate compartments all his life—or at any rate I think he did. Perhaps he was the better satirist for this curious division in his personality. And perhaps, as a consequence of it, Miss Savage, " Madame " and Pauli all got more or less what they wanted of him— and he, of two of them.

Although Butler never " loved " Eliza Mary Ann Savage (What a name !), he was deeply attached to her—just how deeply he realised only when she was dead. His debt to her, human as well as literary, was prodigious. He wanted somebody to whom he could let off—to put the most unfavourable face upon it—all his spite ; for when he had let it off, but only then, he was able to feel thoroughly amiable. Miss Savage was his receptacle for his unpleasant emotions, as well as the confidant of his hopes and fears. And there is no doubt that she encouraged him—even in his most outrageous moments, whether he was letting off his spleen at his father or his sisters, or denouncing the whole tribe of Darwinian scientists, or accusing the reviewers of being in a conspiracy to put him down. Perhaps she thought that it was good for him to get all that stuff off his chest ; but, apart from that, she delighted in the stuff, and found in it a happy outlet for her own repressions. When she had swallowed a good big dose of Butler, it seldom passed out of her without some contribution of her own.

It is improbable that, save occasionally—and on those occasions, as her letters show, she gently and humorously told him off—Miss Savage felt any sense of Butler's unkindness to her, such as he was always reproaching himself with while he was editing their correspondence after her death. There is no need at all to pity Miss Savage. She got a great deal out of her friendship with Butler, as much in relation to her own needs and possibilities as he got in his.

In a literary sense, of course, Butler got much more than encouragement from Miss Savage : he got positive help. She not only made him begin *The Way of All Flesh* : she made him go on with it, put him in better humour with it when he felt it was going wrong, and, *enfin*, was father and midwife to it, all in one. She could vie with Butler himself in taking off her own relations. This, for example, is hers.

> " My aunt has a passion for having all the doors and all the windows of the house always open. You can imagine how pleasant that is with this biting North Wind. *We* don't make our visits too long there. My aunt has always a cold, or neuralgia or rheumatism—sometimes all at once—but they are caused by anything except draughts."

She could also produce, and often did produce, moral sentiments entirely after Butler's heart.

> " I have been very unhappy lately. . . . The fact is I have been doing what I don't often do. I have been doing *right*.

And you know when once one sets about doing right what a deal of harm one does, and one can't stop it ; that's the worst—and it gets beyond one's own control. In this case a friend of mine who has a passion for doing right, and who does no end of harm with the greatest self-complacency, was necessarily acquainted with the affair, and I had to restrain her. So I was stubborn, and even violent, and managed her at last. But it shall be a lesson to me."

Miss Savage also loved inverted sayings—" I believe I may also say the thieves have fallen among me "—and she could write a very pretty satirical passage. This one is about a servant at the Ladies' Club she managed.

"Then I had a housemaid, a Scotch widow, of a certain age, who had never been in service before, an intensely stupid, slow, and easily flurried person. She was religious too, and had many scruples concerning the Sabbath. There were three things, however, which she loathed more than breaking the Sabbath— which were, a duster, a scrubbing brush, and a broom—rather necessary things for a housemaid to handle, but which she would never voluntarily touch. Oh the Fiend ! but she is gone—may I never see her more ! She was a widow, and I know what her husband died of—*Dirt*."

There was one occasion on which Butler, lamenting that he had destroyed her early letters to him, said that " perhaps it is because I have lost them that I imagine that they were written with greater care than any that I have received since." Miss Savage promptly retorted as follows :

"And now, my dear Mr. Butler, let me give you a little good advice. If you wish to make yourself agreeable to the female sex, never hint to a woman that she writes or has written ' with care.' Nothing enrages her so much, and it is only the exceptional sweetness of my disposition that enables me, with some effort, I confess, to forgive this little blunder on your part."

Butler apologised, much more heavily than the occasion demanded, for being " stupid and clumsy." This is one of the points where one gets the feeling that, much as he got out of Miss Savage and enjoyed their relations, he was never quite at his ease about her. The haunting fear that she might, after all, marry him, was never quite absent from his mind, though he exaggerated this feeling later, and it became almost as much an obsession with him as his belief that his father was always trying to put him down. There is in the notes Butler made about Miss Savage and in the sonnets that he wrote about her after her death a quite extraordinary conflict of emotions. She was " incomparably the best and most brilliant woman " he had ever known ; but he said also that she " oppressed me with her very brilliancy—nay bored me, for there is no bore like a brilliant bore." He cried out " how far fuller measure of good things she had meted out to me than I had meted out to her in return " ; but he also wrote that " she rarely left my rooms without my neck swelling, and my head for a time being all wrong, from the effort that it cost me to conceal the fact that she had been too much for me." In his note-books he said again that Miss Savage " haunted " him ; and he was always upbraiding himself for having treated her cavalierly and ill. And then, in the middle of such a confession, he would turn in self-defence against her, accuse her of having laid siege to him, and write unbelievably caddish things about her. Even more than what he said about his father do his *postmortems* on his relations with Miss Savage reveal the deep-down abnormality of his mind—or perhaps one should say rather the nearness to the surface of parts of the mind which in normal men stay usually below the level of consciousness.

He ended his long note on Miss Savage, written in 1885

and revised in 1897—when he was seriously ill—with these
words :

> " Add to this that if I had given her all she would have had
> me give her—I mean if I had married her—nay it was absurd.
> I should have married her in cold blood, not because I wanted
> to marry her, but because she wanted me to marry her."

To the final phrase of this remarkable *confessio* Butler
added in the last year of his life the words " With most
men this is sufficient " : otherwise, he let the passage stand.
I find it inconceivable that the various phrases I have quoted
were written at or near the same time. The more generous
were written mainly in the first reaction after attending
Miss Savage's funeral : the more depreciatory must have
been heavily retouched, if they were not mainly written,
at a much later date. There is no doubt something in
Butler's assertion that Miss Savage " bored " him, and
doubtless he really thought at times that she " loved teasing
and worrying " him ; for people who like, or love, each
other deeply do harbour such thoughts. But that this was
what he *mainly* felt about her at any time during her life
I am quite unable to believe—unless of course one counts
periods of nervous illness, when one can think *anything*. He
worried himself into this defensive counter-attack on her
long after she was dead, because, as he said, she " haunted "
him, and ghosts that do not know when to go are bores.
He wrote in his note-book, in 1895, that Miss Savage
haunted him every day of his life. " I do not suppose a
day ever passes but it comes up to me with a stab that these
people [Miss Savage and a friend named Moorhouse, whom
he felt he had treated badly] were kinder and better friends
to me than I to them." It should perhaps be added that in
November 1897, when he revised the passage about Miss

8

Savage, Butler was actually near a nervous breakdown. The note, as he then revised it, reflects a part of him which was always there, under the skin, but came uppermost only when he was ill. It can by no means be taken as the whole truth, even as he saw it in his more reasonable moments.

Yet it was a facet of the truth ; for Butler was uneasy in most of his friendships, until he settled down with the adoring Festing Jones ready to play with him at a minute's notice any game he wanted to play. Festing Jones, someone has said—I think it was Desmond MacCarthy, who knew them both—was " saturated " in Butler. His careful, endlessly minute biography shows this ; and there is no doubt that Butler loved it all the time. He also thoroughly enjoyed, and had much affection for, his queer man-servant, Alfred, who was the only person who could rebuke him with impunity—unless " Madame " could, but I think she did not try. Butler did not " mind " Alfred, precisely because there was no question of intellectual equality between them. Festing Jones, who had an intellect, never gave Butler anything to mind. He adopted him as " hero " so thoroughly that even Butler could not find fault with him. Towards all the rest of the world Butler had a " temper " which he could usually give vent to, because of his natural timidity in the flesh, only on paper. He bottled it up ; and it sometimes came out sour. As for what he said, a dozen years after they were parted, of Miss Savage—Butler should have been the first to realise that most of us tell our worst lies when we are being " thoroughly frank."

CHAPTER VII

LE STYLE, C'EST L'HOMME

FOR the most part, Butler was a slow writer and an inveterate reviser of what he wrote. He liked too, even if he did not revise his writings, to keep them by him and look at them again after an interval before he let them go. He told Miss Savage, " I am not to be trusted to write three lines unless I can keep them three weeks." The notes which he made in the " little note-books " he was firmly convinced every good author should have always handy he revised persistently, taking immense pains to get the phrases that would say exactly what he meant. Yet he had a great admiration for spontaneous fine writing, when he could find it, as in his prime favourites—Shakespeare, and the authoress of the *Odyssey*. He said that Shakespeare's *Sonnets* were full of " slovenliness, crabbedness and obscurity " ;

> " He [Shakespeare] thought he would take more pains and polish up *Venus and Adonis* and *Lucrece* with extreme care—with what result ? We can admire these last, but we do not want them ; whereas we can read the *Sonnets* over and over and over again."

This was in a letter, in which he went on to adjure his correspondent " not to trouble about a style—not the least little bit."

It was, indeed, not about what he regarded as " style " that Butler did trouble, but about making sure that he was saying what he meant. He wrote in his note-book, " I never

knew a writer yet who took the smallest pains with his style
and was at the same time readable." He continued, after a
gibe at Plato, whom he disliked,

> " A man may, and ought to, take a great deal of pains to
> write clearly, tersely and euphemistically : he will write many
> a sentence three or four times over—to do more than this is
> worse than not rewriting at all : he will be at great pains to
> see that he does not repeat himself, to arrange his matter in
> the way that shall best enable the reader to master it, to cut
> out superfluous words and, even more, to eschew irrelevant
> matter : but in each case he will be thinking not of his own
> style but of his reader's convenience. . . . I should like to put
> it on record that I never took the smallest pains with my style,
> have never thought about it, and do not know or want to
> know whether it is a style at all or whether it is not, as I believe
> and hope, just common, simple straightforwardness. I cannot
> conceive how any man can take thought for his style without
> loss to himself and his readers."

This is all right, up to a point ; but it misses out an
essential element. Butler may not have bothered about
" style," as Newman or Stevenson, whom he mentioned
disparagingly on that account, did bother ; but, equally
with them, he certainly bothered about word and phrase.
He took great pains to find the word he wanted—which
was the word with the right tone of association—and to
get his key phrases into a telling shape. The line between
doing this and bothering about " style " is not easy to draw.
What Butler really meant was that he liked his style to be
" penny plain," and not " twopence coloured " ; but that
did not in fact make it less a style. He could not bear
ornateness, which he took to imply artificiality : whereas
he saw nothing artificial in hunting round meticulously for
the right phrase.

The consequence is that Butler has quite unmistakeably a style. He once called his translations of Homer " Tottenham Court Road," as contrasted with Butcher and Lang's " Wardour Street." But no one can read his versions without realising that " Tottenham Court Road," fully as much as " Wardour Street," is a style.

> " Calypso trembled with rage when she heard this. ' You gods,' she exclaimed, ' ought to be ashamed of yourselves. You are always jealous, and hate seeing a goddess take a fancy to a mortal man, and live with him in open matrimony. . . . And now you are angry with me too because I have a man here. I found the poor creature sitting all alone astride of a keel, for Jove had struck his ship with lightning and sunk it in mid ocean, so that all his crew were drowned, while he himself was driven by wind and waves on to my island. I got fond of him and cherished him, and had set my heart on making him immortal, so that he should never grow old all his days ; still I cannot curse Jove, nor bring his counsels to nothing : therefore, if he insists upon it, let the man go beyond the seas again."

This is certainly not much like the *Odyssey* ; for the *Odyssey* is poetry first and foremost. But, no less certainly, it has a style, and gets, by that style, precisely the effect it aims at. Butler elsewhere endorsed the epigram " *Le style c'est l'homme,*" and said that " the personality of the author is what interests me more than his work." Butler's personality got into everything he wrote—even when he was only translator—and it got in, not only because of the characteristicness of what he was saying, but also because of the way he said it. If that is not having a style, I do not know what is.

Butler said this too. " A man's style in any art should be like his dress—it should attract as little attention as possible." In dress and manner, he lived up to that principle ;

and he did so in his style as well—if for " attract " we may
read " distract." The " style " Butler disliked was that
which either diverts attention away from the matter, or
renders it obscure. He insisted on the utmost plainness—
as every satirist should—for the satirist gets his best effects
from being bald. The best way of stripping his victims
naked is to take off all literary clothes. So many follies and
hypocrisies yield up their inwardness at once when there is
nothing left—not even a superfluous word—to cover them
up. Butler knew this well, or at all events wrote as if he
knew it. He was as plain as Defoe, and a great deal more
honest. For Defoe often used apparent plainness as a means
of mystification, whereas Butler never meant to make a
mystery of anything. He hated mysteries, except as problems
that he could put his wits to clearing up.

Of such a writer there will be always two opinions ; for
the world divides itself between the lovers of " twopence
coloured " and of " penny plain." The colourings men like
are infinitely various, and the tastes in them change with
the frequency of fashion. The unfashionable colouring is
always anathema. The " penny plain," though there are
always many who dislike it, wears better, because there is
less in it of stuck-on adornment, and it is more in the texture
of the writing itself. Happy the man who has a plain style
that is a style, and not merely a flatness. He will, almost
of necessity, be a master of phrase, and a fine judge of
words and their associations ; for it is through phrases
and through the associations of words that he will get
his effects.

Butler was a painter and a musician, as well as a writer.
He said of his painting : " If I had gone on doing things out
of my own head, instead of making studies, I should have

been all right." He was convinced that what had gone wrong with his painting was that he had been academic about it, and had tried to follow other people's notions, instead of expressing his own. He made the remark just quoted in relation to his painting "Family Prayers," in which he was saying something definite, and of his own— on a theme which was close to that of *The Way of All Flesh*. This was an early picture, painted before he had fallen into the bad habit of trying to paint what the judges of the Royal Academy would accept. When they rejected his pictures, he gave up trying to be a successful painter, and went on only with water-colours—mostly landscapes—for which he had a small talent. "Family Prayers," which has a definite style of its own, makes one half regret that his painting went awry ; but he was probably right in saying that he had done better in literature than he would ever have done as a painter, even if he had been " all right."

As for his music, I have never heard any of it, and cannot judge. It was all, he himself said, based on Handel, the only composer for whom he ever really cared. But it was evidently, in conception at any rate, very much his own ; and he did not make the mistake of " making studies " in order to perfect himself in the art of composition. He learnt what he had to learn, in order to compose at all in Handel's manner ; and then he let himself go, getting great fun out of making appropriate music about the " horrid fiend," Speculation, and later out of " the monster, Polypheme," in *Ulysses*. Nobody that I am aware of has ever suggested that Butler was a great composer, and he had no notion of it himself. But it is true that his command of the arts of painting and music, inferior as these accomplish- ments were to his talent as a writer, contributed to his literary quality. He heard what he was writing, and saw the shape of what he set out to describe.

Besides being prose-writer, painter and musician, Butler was a poet; and his poetry is one of the queerest things about him. Most people know his *Psalm of Montreal*, with its famous refrain " O God ! O Montreal ! " and its picture of the " Discobolus " tucked away in a lumber room of the Montreal Museum with an old man stuffing an owl for company. Most people remember a few lines at least :

> " And I turned to the man of skins and said unto him, ' O thou
> man of skins,
> Wherefore hast thou done thus to shame the beauty of the
> Discobolus ? '
> But the Lord had hardened the heart of the man of skins
> And he answered, ' My brother-in-law is haberdasher to Mr.
> Spurgeon.' "

Few people read *A Psalm of Montreal* without liking it ; but some say that it is not poetry. Butler, however, can claim some place as a poet on other accounts. His farewell to Hans Faesch is true poetry.[1] It begins—

> " Out, out, out into the night
> With the wind bitter North-East and the sea rough :
> You have a racking cough and your lungs are weak,
> But out, out into the night you go,
> So guide you and guard you Heaven, and fare you well."

So are some of his sonnets real poetry, written greatly under Shakespeare's influence—especially that which begins " Not on sad Stygian shore " and ends

> " Yet meet we shall, and part, and meet again,
> Where dead men meet, on lips of living men."

---

[1] Quoted in full in H. Festing Jones's *Life*, Vol. II, p. 201.

Finally, Butler was a person who put himself—or a great deal of himself—into his writing. He did not, however, put all of himself—even if his letters and his note-books are included in the account. There is always something of an enigma about him—which explains why books about Butler's books have to be largely books about Butler. There was something pathological in his attitude, not only to his father but also to Miss Savage, and equally in his mingling of speculative boldness with timidity in action, and of hard hits at his enemies with a certain running away from life and an acute sensibility even to mild slaps directed at himself.

> So here's to Mr. Butler, who fascinated Shaw,
> Who wrote a first-rate novel, and left it in a drawer.
> With very little science, and not a deal of Greek,
> He saw ahead of Darwin, and made the scholars squeak.

APPENDICES

I. SAMUEL BUTLER'S BOOKS

1863. *A First Year in Canterbury Settlement.*

1865. *The Evidence for the Resurrection of Jesus Christ as given by the Four Evangelists critically examined.* (Pamphlet.)

1872. *Erewhon, or, Over the Range.*

1873. *The Fair Haven.*

1877. *Life and Habit.* (Dated 1878.)

1879. *Evolution Old and New.*

1880. *Unconscious Memory.*

1881. *Alps and Sanctuaries of Piedmont and the Canton Ticino.*

1884. *Selections from Previous Works,* with Remarks on Romanes's "Mental Evolution in Animals," and "A Psalm of Montreal."

1885. *Gavottes, Minuets, Fugues, and Other Short Pieces for the Piano* (with H. Festing Jones).

1886. *Luck or Cunning ?*

1888. *Ex Voto. Narcissus,* an Oratorio (with H. Festing Jones).

1892. *The Humour of Homer.* (Pamphlet.)

1893. *On the Trapanese Origin of the Odyssey.* (Pamphlet.)

1896. *The Life and Letters of Dr. Samuel Butler.*

1897. *The Authoress of the Odyssey.*

1898. *The Iliad of Homer rendered into English Prose.*

1899. *Shakespeare's Sonnets Reconsidered.*

1900. *The Odyssey rendered into English Prose.*

1901. *Erewhon Revisited.*

1903. *The Way of All Flesh.*

1904. *Essays in Life, Art and Science. Ulysses, a Cantata* (with H. Festing Jones), *Seven Sonnets and A Psalm of Montreal.* (Privately printed.)

1909. *God the Known and God the Unknown.*

1912. *The Note-Books of Samuel Butler.*

1913. *The Humour of Homer, and Other Essays.*

1932. *Butleriana.* (Nonesuch Press.)

1935. *Letters between Samuel Butler and Miss Savage.*

II. A BRIEF BIOGRAPHICAL NOTE

1835.   Born, December 4.

1843.   First visit to Italy.

1846–48. School at Allesley, near Coventry.

1848–54. School at Shrewsbury.

1853.   Second visit to Italy (and many thereafter).

1854.   Goes up to St. John's College, Cambridge.

1858.   Bracketed twelfth in Classical Tripos.

1858–59. Contributes to *The Eagle* (College magazine).
Works in London parish and prepares for ordination.
Takes lessons in drawing.

1859.   Refuses to be ordained.
Emigrates to Canterbury Settlement, New Zealand.

1860–64. Studies Darwin and Christian evidences in New Zealand.
Contributes to New Zealand *Press* on Darwinism.

1863.   Meets Charles Paine Pauli.

1864.   Returns to England with Pauli, and settles in Clifford's Inn.
Sets to work to be a painter. Paints "Family Prayers."

1867.   Meets Miss Savage at Heatherley's School of Art.

1869–76. Exhibits at Royal Academy.

1870.   Begins writing *Erewhon*.

1871.   Extant correspondence with Miss Savage begins.

1872.   Meets Lucie Dumas (" Madame "). Begins *The Way of All Flesh*.

1873.   His mother dies. He invests in Hoare's companies.

1874.   Hoare's companies collapse. Goes to Canada (1874–75).

1876.   Begins *Life and Habit*. Meets Henry Festing Jones.

1880.   Quarrels with Darwin.

1880–83. Rewrites *The Way of All Flesh*.

1881.   His money difficulties ended.

1883.   Begins composing music in the style of Handel.

1885.   Death of Miss Savage.

1886.   His father dies, and he becomes well-to-do.

1887.   Engages Alfred Emery Cathie as clerk.

1891.　　Begins translating the *Odyssey* and formulating his Homeric theories.

1892.　　Death of Lucie Dumas.

1893.　　Friendship with Hans Faesch begins.

1896.　　Gogin paints his portrait (now in National Portrait Gallery).

1897.　　Death of Pauli.

1901.　　Writes Sonnets on Miss Savage.

1902.　　Illness and Death (June 18).

III. BOOKS ABOUT BUTLER

Samuel Butler, a Memoir. By HENRY FESTING JONES. Two volumes·
1920.

Samuel Butler and his Family Relations. By Mrs. R. S. GARNETT.
1926.

Samuel Butler. By C. E. M. JOAD. 1924.

Life and Letters. Samuel Butler Number. Edited by Desmond
MacCarthy. October, 1931.

Butleriana. (Nonesuch Press.) 1932.